Misguided G

The Conservative Case against Neoconservatism

Jack Kerwick

Misguided Guardians: The Conservative Case against Neoconservatism

Other books by Jack Kerwick
The American Offensive: Dispatches from the Front

© 2016 Jack Kerwick All Rights Reserved
Print ISBN 978-1-941071-49-6
ebook ISBN 978-1-941071-50-2

This book is sold subject to the condition that it shall not, by way of trade or otherwise, be lent, resold, hired out or otherwise circulated without the publisher's prior consent in any form of binding or cover other than that in which it is published and without a similar condition including this condition being imposed on the subsequent purchaser.

STAIRWAY PRESS—LAS VEGAS

Cover Design by Guy D. Corp
www.GrafixCorp.com

STAIRWAY≡PRESS

www.StairwayPress.com
848 North Rainbow Blvd #5015
Las Vegas, NV 89107 USA

INTRODUCTION

THE EIGHTEENTH CENTURY German philosopher Immanuel Kant is credited with having achieved a Copernican-like revolution in the fields of epistemology and metaphysics. Just as Copernicus inverted the Ptolemaic paradigm of the cosmos by showing that the Earth, far from being stationary, actually revolves around the sun, so too did Kant contend that the mind, far from being a passive receptacle of sensory data that seeks to conform to reality, is an active entity that conforms reality to *itself*. The mind, in other words, doesn't *mirror* reality; it *constructs* it.

The self-avowed guardians of the contemporary "conservative" movement in America are Kantians of a sort. It's not, of course, that they subscribe to Kant's philosophy. Few of them, odds are, have even heard of Kant. Yet these movers and shakers of the "conservative" movement are "Kantians" inasmuch as they've *assimilated* the word "conservatism" to their policy preferences rather than insure that those preferences *reflect* their ostensible commitments to a political philosophy, to something called "conservatism."

"Conservatism" seems nowadays to mean whatever self-identified "conservative" politicians and media personalities want for it to mean.

However, those policy preferences of self-declared "conservatives" for things like massive Third-World immigration, amnesty, socialized medicine of the Medicare and Medicaid varieties, federal "civil rights" laws divesting both the states and individuals of their Constitutional prerogatives, and military adventurism designed to export "liberal democracy" to the proverbial four corners of the globe—though they have nothing whatsoever to do with conservatism as traditionally conceived—are not just a haphazard collection of discrete thoughts. Conjointly, they constitute an ideological template. The ideology, though, is not classical or traditional conservatism.

It is *neoconservatism*.

To put this point another way, most of those in Washington D.C. and the media who speak on behalf of "conservatism" are actually neoconservatives. And between conservatism and neoconservatism there are differences, not just in degree, but in kind. The main objective of this book—a compilation of nine essays that I've had published over the last five years—is to show just this. More specifically, my aim here is to identify not just how conservatism differs philosophically from neoconservatism, but what it has to say vis-à-vis such issues as religion, patriotism, "American Exceptionalism," race and racism, and higher education. Each essay constitutes its own chapter.

In the first chapter, "Conservatism vs. Neoconservatism: A Philosophical Analysis," I delineate the epistemological, metaphysical, ethical, and political-philosophical presuppositions underwriting classical conservatism and contrast these with those presuppositions that inform neoconservatism.

In the second and third chapters—"Conservatism vs. Neoconservatism: Religion and Ideology," and "Conservatism vs. Neoconservatism: Patriotism"—I show how these conflicting philosophical visions result in equally incompatible views on religion and patriotism, respectively.

The fourth, fifth, and sixth chapters explore the variety of respects in which conservative philosophy intersects with race, specifically what is often termed, "black conservatism." Chapter four, "Conservatism and Race: Black Heterodoxy," reveals that what is typically referred to as "black conservatism" actually consists of several strains of heterodoxy, thought that deviates from the standard leftist orthodoxies that predominate among black thinkers. Libertarianism, neoconservatism, and classical conservatism are the varieties of unconventional views to be found among this minority of black writers. That being said, chapter five, "Conservatism and Race: The Philosophy of 'Black Conservative' Thomas Sowell," and chapter six, "Conservatism and Race: The Philosophy of "Black Conservative" George S. Schuyler, establish that conservatism does indeed have its proponents among some black essayists.

Considering that conservatives (along with virtually everyone else who for whatever reasons comes within the crosshairs of the "anti-racists") are not infrequently charged with "racism," in the seventh chapter—"Conservatism and 'Racism:' Deconstructing an Unwieldy Concept"—I subject the concept of "racism" to the interrogation that it has always managed to elude. Here I show that there are actually "racism*s,*" at least four logically distinct conceptions that fail to vindicate the common notion that "racism" is both pervasive and especially awful.

The last two chapters examine the conservative's disposition toward the ideal of a liberal arts education. In the eighth—"Conservatism and Higher Education: Liberal Learning as a Conversation"—it is argued that liberal learning should be conceived along the lines of a dialogue between the past, the present, and the future, the dead, the living, and those not yet born, as Edmund Burke characterized the "social contract." In the final chapter—"Conservatism and Higher Education: 'The Inability to Think' and Moral Goodness"—I contend that in order for college educators to fulfill their traditional vocation to educate both the heads and hearts of their students, yet in order to avoid succumbing to the temptation to politicize curriculum, academics must cultivate the virtue of civility, the art of being *mannerly*. Drawing on the insights of Hannah Arendt, I show that there *is* a relationship between morality and "the ability to think."

Chapter 1 4

CONSERVATISM vs. NEOCONSERVATISM: A PHILOSOPHICAL ANALYSIS 4

    Conservatism 5
    Neoconservatism 9
    Conclusion 16

Chapter 2 17

CONSERVATISM vs. NEOCONSERVATISM: RELIGION AND IDEOLOGY 17

    II 18
    III 23
    Conclusion 31

Chapter 3 33

CONSERVATISM v. NEOCONSERVATISM: PATRIOTISM 33

    Patriotism, Rationalism & Universalism 34
    Neoconservatism 38
    Conservatism 42
    The Universal and the Particular 45
    Conclusion 51

Chapter 4 52

CONSERVATISM AND RACE: "BLACK HETERODOXY" 52

    Introduction 52
    Classical Conservatism 53
    George S. Schuyler 56
    Thomas Sowell 62
    Classical Liberalism 66
    Walter E. Williams 67
    Neoconservatism 70
    Alan Keyes 73
    Conclusion 76

Chapter 5 78

CONSERVATISM and RACE: THE PHILOSOPHY OF "BLACK CONSERVATIVE" THOMAS SOWELL 78

    Introduction 78
    II 79
    III 91

Conclusion 103
Chapter 6 105
CONSERVATISM and RACE: THE PHILOSOPHY OF "BLACK CONSERVATIVE" GEORGE S. SCHUYLER 105

    Introduction 105
    Rationalism 107
    Reason and Knowledge 107
    Ethics & Political Philosophy 108
    Blackism 109
    Conservatism 114
    Reason & Knowledge 114
    Morality and Political Philosophy 115
    George S. Schuyler 116
    Conclusion 124

Chapter 7 125
CONSERVATISM AND "RACISM": DECONSTRUCTING AN UNWIELDY CONCEPT 125

    Introduction 125
    Exposition on "Racism" as "Racial Hatred" 126
    Critique 127
    Exposition on "Racism" as "Racial Discrimination" 130
    Critique 131
    Exposition on "Racism" as Doctrine of "Innate Inferiority" (II) 134
    Critique 134
    Exposition on "Racism" as "Institutional Racism" 136
    Critique 137
    Some Objections and Counter-Objections 140
    Conclusion 142

Chapter 8 143
CONSERVATISM AND HIGHER EDUCATION: LIBERAL LEARNING AS A *CONVERSATION* 143

    Introduction 143
    Traditionalism 143
    Careerism 145

    Activism 146
    The Conversational Ideal: Education as a Conversation.. 147
    Conclusion 151
Chapter 9... 152
CONSERVATISM AND HIGHER EDUCATION: THE
"INABILITY TO THINK" AND MORAL GOODNESS 152
    The Ideology of the Academy and the Culture 154
    The Inability to Think 157
    Civility 158
    Conclusion 159
ENDNOTES.. 161

Jack Kerwick

Chapter 1

CONSERVATISM vs. NEOCONSERVATISM: A PHILOSOPHICAL ANALYSIS

ACCORDING TO THE conventional wisdom among self-declared representatives of "the conservative movement," William F. Buckley is "the master"[1] to whom conservatives owe an eternal debt of gratitude for expunging from their ranks the dregs—the "racists," the "anti-Semites," and "extremists" of all sorts—that threatened the movement's social respectability.[2]

This account, however, isn't *history* at all. It is ideology or politics taking refuge behind the value-neutral guise of history.[3] In reality, "the conservative movement" has long since been a predominantly *neoconservative* movement. While there is plenty of historical, sociological, and polemical literature on neoconservatism, there is relatively little that treats it *philosophically*. Yet, as I will show, neoconservatism *is* indeed a distinctive philosophical theory inasmuch as it consists of conceptions of knowledge, ethics, and the state that differ in kind from those underlying traditional conservatism. Moreover, neoconservatism is an expression of *Rationalism*, exactly that orientation against which conservatives have been railing since at least the time of Burke.

My method here is simple enough. First, I look at such figures as Edmund Burke, Russell Kirk, and Michael Oakeshott to reveal what I take to be a distinctive set of philosophical presuppositions that has informed conservative thought for more than 200 years.[4] Then, I identify an assortment of scholarly and popular writers alike—from Leo Strauss, Alan Bloom, and Irving Kristol, to William Bennett, Douglas Murray, Charles Krauthammer, Dennis Prager, and Michael Medved—ranging over the last half of a century who disclose both that neoconservatism is indeed its own intellectual tradition *and* that it is antithetical to conservatism.[5]

Conservatism

Edmund Burke distinguished himself as "the patron saint of conservatism" via his *Reflections on the Revolution in France*. Yet while it was upon the Revolution that he specifically set his sights, it was the Rationalist philosophy animating the revolution that Burke brought out into the open and blasted to bits.

Reason, on this score, is supra-historical. It must, then, seek to emancipate itself from the *traditions* that have enslaved it from time immemorial, for reason is both a universal and a unitary phenomenon: it is universal insofar as there are no problems that it cannot, in principle, rectify; it is unitary inasmuch as all minds properly trained in its exercise should coincide when both identifying and solving problems.

To be clear, from the standpoint of Reason, the contingencies and relativities of time and place are burdensome encumbrances. Reason is resolutely impartial with respect to those particularities that individuate peoples and engage their affections. To its tribunal, then, all traditions—the merely concrete, the local, the transitory—must yield.

Against this rationalist epistemology Burke articulated another. His rationalist he referred to as "political-theologians" and "theological-politicians,"[6] "new doctors of the rights of men,"[7] "moral politicians,"[8] "men of theory,"[9] "levelers,"[10] peddlers of a "mechanic philosophy,"[11] of an "empire of light and reason."[12] Reason, Burke insisted, does not exist in advance of all tradition; to no slight extent, it is a by-product of the latter.

"We are afraid to put men to live and trade each on his own private stock of reason," Burke famously states, for "we suspect that the stock in each man is small, and that the individual would do better to avail himself of the general bank and capital of nations and of ages." He then draws his audience's attention to what he perceives to be the fundamental difference between the conservative conception of knowledge on behalf of which he argues and that of the rationalist conception that he rejects. "Many of our men of speculation," Burke asserts, "instead of exploding general prejudices, employ their sagacity to discover the latent wisdom which prevails in them."[13] Then, rather than "cast away the coat of prejudice" in favor of "the naked reason," the wise retain the prejudice, for it alone supplies a "motive to give action to that reason, and an affection which will give it permanence."[14]

Notice, knowledge is, to a significant degree (though certainly not exclusively) *inarticulate,* the fruits of the experiences of generations over centuries and millennia. Moreover, because this knowledge is passed on from "those who are dead" to "those who are living" and "those who are to be born,"[15] it is constituted by *tradition.* That is, contrary to what rationalists imply, reason cannot discard tradition without discarding itself.

The conservative's tradition-based epistemology is inseparable from his tradition-based vision of morality. Morality is largely a matter of observing "ancient indisputable laws and liberties," age-old cultural customs that Burke urges us to view as "*an entailed inheritance,*" a thousand generations' worth of social capital.[16] In habituating ourselves to the "manners" and "moral opinions" of our ancestors,[17] by learning "to love" the local and concrete institutions, "the little platoon(s)," [18] we succeed in cultivating "those inbred sentiments which are the faithful guardians, the active monitors of our duty," and "the true supporters of all liberal and manly morals." [19]

The Rationalist's moral philosophy, in stark contrast, is just as abstract as his epistemology. The moral life consists not in the observance of traditional customs, as it does for the conservative, but in the advancement of *principles* (or, in a later idiom, "*values*") like "the rights of men." [20] The latter are supposed to be "self-evident." A morality of abstract, universal principles can only condemn as a moral *failure* the kind of partiality toward one's own demanded by a morality of tradition.

"Against" the rights of men, Burke says, "there can be no prescription; against these no argument is binding: these admit no temperament and no compromise: anything withheld from their full demand is so much of fraud and injustice." He continues: "Against these their rights of men let no government look for security in the length of its continuance, or in the justice and lenity of its administration." If reality fails to "quadrate with their theories [of the rights of men]," then the oldest and most "beneficent government" is as susceptible as "the most violent tyranny" of being toppled.[21] The Rationalist's "rights of men" Burke refers to as "pretended rights," "extremes" that, "in proportion as they are metaphysically true...are morally and politically false." [22]

The Rationalist's conception of morality informs his view of the state as an "enterprise association," to quote Michael Oakeshott. When the state is treated as such, its members are regarded as being "related to one another in terms of their *joint pursuit* of some recognized *substantive purpose*," a pursuit in which they are "obligated to engage [.]" [23] An enterprise association is a type of association "in which a Many becomes One [.]" [24] Associates are all "servants of the purpose" that distinguishes and justifies their existence while the government assumes the form of "a managerial engagement." [25]

Burke charges his Rationalist opponents with approaching "the science of constructing a commonwealth, or renovating it, or reforming it," as if it could be known "*a priori*." A state, he notes, has "various ends" that "admit of infinite modifications" that can't be "settled" by appeal to "any abstract rule" or "principle." [26] The Rationalist, viewing society as if it had but a "single end," fails to recognize that "the objects of society are of the greatest possible complexity [.]" This being so, the Rationalist is fundamentally mistaken in believing that a "simple disposition or direction of power can be suitable either to man's nature or to the quality of his affairs." [27]

The conservative tends to treat the state as a *civil* association. Here, associates "are related solely in respect to their obligations to observe" the *law*. Unlike the *policies* of an enterprise association, laws do *not* "specify a practice or routine purporting to promote the achievement of a substantive purpose." [28] Members of civil association are not joint-enterprisers conscripted in the service of realizing a common goal. Their enterprises, rather, are self-chosen. In other words, they are not told *what* they must do, but only *how* they must do whatever it is that they choose to do. And the government of such an association is not a manager, but more like an umpire, the "custodian of the rules [.]" [29]

Russell Kirk, whose death, William F. Buckley claimed, "left the conservative community desolate," [30] articulates the conservative vision succinctly. The conservative, Kirk notes, regards as utopian folly "*a priori* designs for perfecting human nature and society," [31] the "fanatical ideological dogmata" [32] of "metaphysical enthusiasts" [33] who refuse to grasp that principles are "arrived at by convention and compromise, for the most part, and tested by long experience." [34] Kirk contrasts the conservative's "affection for the proliferating variety and mystery of human existence" with the "uniformity, egalitarianism, and utilitarianism of most radical systems," [35] and his "faith in prescription" with the certitude of those Rationalists "who would reconstruct society along abstract designs." [36]

The conservative's philosophy of change reflects his commitment to tradition. Appearing "always...as deprivation," [37] change "is an emblem of extinction." [38] Thus, with an eye toward assimilating change, Burke characterized the English Constitution in terms of "an inheritance from our forefathers [.]" Such an image, in linking the present generation with its "forefathers" and its "posterity," "preserves an unity in so great a diversity of its parts," [39] thus guaranteeing "a condition of unchangeable constancy [.]" [40] The image of an inheritance assures that "change will proceed by insensible degrees" and along a "gradual course...." [41]

Kirk adds that change should "come as the consequence of a need generally felt, not inspired by fine-spun abstractions." The trick is to discriminate between "a profound, slow, natural alteration," on the one hand, and, on the other, "some infatuation of the hour." Rationalists are ineligible to be "agents of change," for "the perceptive reformer" knows that "an ability to reform" must be reconciled "with a disposition to preserve[.]" [42]

As we shall now see, neoconservatism shares none of the philosophical suppositions of conservatism. In fact, epistemologically, metaphysically, ethically, and political-philosophically, neoconservatism is a species of Rationalism through and through.

Neoconservatism

There are few self-avowed "conservatives" today that aren't, to some measure or other, actually *neo*conservatives. Interestingly, though, there are even fewer people who are ready to regard the label of "neoconservatism" as anything other than an ad hominem attack, even an "anti-Semitic" epithet.[43] Still, it *has* its apologists, most of whom are all too ready to concede that "socially, economically, and philosophically," neoconservatism differs in kind from traditional conservatism. Some of its proponents even admit that the former is the antithesis of the latter in being "revolutionary [.]"[44]

We should begin with the 20th century philosopher Leo Strauss, "a useful and necessary point of entry for any investigation of neoconservatism."[45] Strauss affirms "natural right" on the ground that, without it, we have nothing but "blind choice" for our actions.[46] Unlike Burke and conservatives generally, Strauss is convinced that the only alternative to natural right is "positive right," that which "is determined exclusively by the legislators and courts of the various countries."[47]

No one is clearer on the differences between Strauss and Burke than Strauss himself. First, the latter charges the former and other "eminent conservatives" with being "historicists" for their reliance upon tradition and their disavowal of such "universal or abstract principles" like natural rights. Strauss realizes what conservatives realize, that these principles have "necessarily a revolutionary, disturbing, [and] unsettling effect" upon a country in that they "prevent men from wholeheartedly identifying themselves with, or accepting, the social order that fate has allotted them."[48] Secondly, Strauss equates Burke's rejection of the Rationalist's notion of Reason with "a certain depreciation of reason"[49] per se. This, Strauss thinks, accounts for why Burke passes over "the [general] view that constitutions can be 'made' in favor of the view that they must 'grow,'" and the specific belief "that the best social order can be or ought to be the work of an individual, of a wise 'legislator' or founder."[50]

We must grasp something here: Strauss' and Burke's beliefs concerning the origins of constitutions reveal their conflicting beliefs regarding the kind of association, "civil" or "enterprise," that a modern state should be. This difference between the neoconservative and conservative visions becomes clearer yet when we turn to the thought of Strauss's student, Allan Bloom.

In his *The Closing of the American Mind,* Bloom writes that America "is one of the highest and most extreme achievements of the rational quest for the good life according to nature," a "regime" guaranteeing "untrammeled freedom to reason." The American "regime" is grounded in "the rational principles of natural right" alone.[51] It is to these "rational principles" that the American patriot is committed and in the light of which "class, race, religion, national origin," and "culture all disappear or become dim[.]"[52] America, the "liberal democracy" par excellence, is "the regime of equality and liberty, of the rights of man," "the regime of reason."[53]

If there were any doubts that neoconservatism is a brand of Rationalism, the quotations from Bloom should suffice to dispel them once and for all. Here we have it: morality consists in abstract, universal principles of natural right—*not* the historically embodied experience of "nations and of ages," as Burke put it. The principles of natural right upon which America is said to have been founded, like the Reason to which they are "self-evident," are independent of the contingencies of time and place. And because America is "the regime" that embodies them most fully, it has a special—an "exceptional"—responsibility to promote them throughout the world by promoting "liberal democracy."

Irving Kristol is known as "the godfather" of neoconservatism, a distinction that he happily accepts. Kristol is quick to dispatch the objection that the relationship between Strauss and neoconservatism has been, at best, exaggerated. Among "neoconservative intellectuals" he identifies Strauss by name[54] and credits him with, among other things, supplying Kristol and his ideological ilk with their "favorite neoconservative text on foreign affairs," Thucydides on the Peloponnesian War.[55]

Neoconservatism, Kristol informs us, endorses "the welfare state" in that its adherents support "social security, unemployment insurance, some form of national health insurance, some kind of family assistance plan, etc., " and it will not hesitate "to interfere with the market for overriding social purposes"—even if this requires "'rigging'" instead of imposing upon it "direct bureaucratic controls." [56]

Neoconservatives accept "the equality of natural rights" enshrined in the Declaration of Independence[57] and view them as "the principles of" America's "establishment," [58] the principles of "the universal creed" upon which the nation is "based." [59] The United States, then, is "a creedal nation" [60] with a "'civilizing mission'" [61] to promote "American values" [62] throughout the world, to see to it "that other governments respect our conception of individual rights as the foundation of a just regime and a good society." Kristol is unambiguous: the United States, given its status as a "great power" and its "ideological" nature, does indeed have a responsibility, "in those places and at those times where conditions permit" it "to flourish," to "'make the world safe for democracy." [63]

The "godfather" of neoconservatism is clear that, both domestically and globally, his ideology looks upon the United States as, in Oakeshott's words, an "enterprise association." America has a vocation, first and foremost, to export the "values" of "democracy" to the rest of the world. This is the grand enterprise to which all citizens are expected to deploy at least some of their resources. Other resources must be marshaled for the sake of fulfilling purposes right here at home. As Kristol says, neoconservatives are "always interested in proposing alternate reforms, alternate legislation, [to the Great Society] that would achieve *the desired aims*"—the eradication of poverty—"more securely, and without the downside effects." [64] Neoconservatives don't want to "destroy the welfare state, but…rather reconstruct it along more economical and humane lines." [65]

While many contemporary neoconservatives deny it, Kristol is blunt regarding the marked differences between neoconservatism and conservatism. "Neocons," he states, "feel at home in today's America to a degree that more traditional conservative do not." ⁶⁶ Neoconservatism is the first "variant" of conservatism to be "in the American grain." This is because it is "hopeful, not lugubrious; forward-looking, not nostalgic; and its general tone is cheerful, not grim or dyspeptic." But there's more. "Its twentieth-century heroes tend to be TR [Teddy Roosevelt], FDR [Franklin Delano Roosevelt], and Ronald Reagan," while "Republican and conservative worthies" like "Calvin Coolidge, Herbert Hoover, Dwight Eisenhower, and Barry Goldwater are politely overlooked." ⁶⁷

That "the conservative movement" retains this distinctly neoconservative character to the present day can be easily gotten from the comments of some of its leading lights. Take, for instance, William J. Bennett, a former cabinet member of the administrations of Presidents Reagan and Bush Sr. who is now a nationally syndicated talk radio host. Bennett articulates as clearly as anyone the neoconservative's conviction that morality requires subscription to abstract, self-evident principles or ideals, and that the (American) state has a commitment to advance these values throughout the world. American patriotism demands "steadfast devotion to the ideals of freedom and equality," Bennett insists. The Founders discovered "something quite new—a new nation conceived in a new way and dedicated to a new self-evident truth that all men are created equal," Bennett explains. America is "a country tied together in loyalty to a principle [.]" ⁶⁸

Fox News celebrity and nationally syndicated columnist Charles Krauthammer locates himself unmistakably within this neoconservative intellectual tradition when he describes America as "a nation uniquely built not on blood, race or consanguinity, but on *a proposition*"—the proposition that all human beings are created equal, or possess equal rights. Krauthammer, along with his fellow neoconservatives, refer to this creed as "American exceptionalism." From it, he makes the characteristically neoconservative move and deduces a "value-driven foreign policy"—what he calls "democratic globalism." From the latter vantage point, "the engine of history" is "not the will to power but the will to freedom" [69]—i.e. "the spread of democracy" around the planet.[70]

Democratic globalism Krauthammer contrasts with three other approaches to foreign policy: "isolationism," "liberal internationalism," and "realism." The first he rejects for being "an ideology of fear." It promotes and reflects "fear of trade," "immigrants," "the Other." "Isolationists" favor "pulling up the drawbridge to Fortress America." [71] The problem with "liberal internationalism," as Krauthammer sees it, is that it stresses "multilateralism," which in turn threatens "to blunt the pursuit of American national interests by making them subordinate to a myriad of other interests[.]" [72] "Realism" defines "interest" in terms of "power," and we "cannot live by power alone," for "America's national interest" is "an expression of values." [73]

And this is just how it is viewed from the perspective of Krauthammer's "democratic globalism." The latter "can teach realism...that the spread of democracy is not just an end but a means, an indispensable means for securing American interests." [74] In other words, the more "democracies" in the world the more secure is America.

Krauthammer is quick to note that the "universalism" of democratic globalism, "its open-ended commitment to human freedom, its temptation to plant the flag of democracy everywhere," poses a real "danger[.]" To guard against this, Krauthammer proposes the "axiom" of what he calls "democratic *realism.*" Democratic realism supplies a criterion for the use of American force. While America:

> ...will support democracy everywhere...

...it...

> ...will commit blood and treasure only in places where there is a strategic necessity,

...i.e. ...

> ...*places central to the larger war against the existential enemy, the enemy that poses a global mortal threat to freedom.* [75]

The vast majority of Krauthammer's colleagues among the "conservative" punditry class agree with him precisely on all of these points. Nationally syndicated columnist and radio show host Dennis Prager, for instance, affirms "American exceptionalism" while explaining that it is nothing more or less than the belief that "America often knows better than the world what is right and wrong." And why is this? For the most part, belief in "American exceptionalism" rises from the "Judeo-Christian" character of America's "values." [76] Though these "values" have going for them their "moral superiority" to all others, they are also of "universal applicability" and "eminently exportable." Prager is unabashed: "These magnificent American values are applicable to virtually every society in the world."

Syndicated columnist and radio show host Michael Medved responds to the charge that "conservatives" like himself reveal inconsistencies in their thought when they simultaneously contend for less intrusive government at home *and* a more "activist" American government abroad. The solution to this apparent inconsistency, Medved insists, turns on the view of "American exceptionalism" held by "conservatives" who "passionately embrace the idea that the United States is better than the rest of the world," the "almost mystical faith in the American people and the powers of the market." Thus, since Americans "need a strong hand from Washington far less than do beleaguered hordes in less fortunate societies around the world," there should be "less Washington interference at home and more Washington determination abroad [.]" [77]

Neoconservatism, it should now be clear, endorses

conceptions of knowledge, morality, and political philosophy that are unmistakably *rationalist* in character. Reason is a universal faculty based on abstract moral principles, ideals or values. Since it is for the sake of realizing these eternal moral verities, both home and abroad, that the American state exists, America, from this perspective, is seen as an "enterprise association," an association defined in terms of its *goals*.

Conclusion

By now I hope to have persuaded the reader of the truth of two theses. First, contrary to what its name and adherents would have us believe, neoconservatism is most emphatically *not* just another variation of conservatism, a species of conservative thought distinguished on account of its *emphases*. Rather, neoconservatism is a reasonably coherent philosophy comprised of epistemological, metaphysical, ethical, and political-philosophical suppositions that differ *in kind* from those that inform the classical conservative tradition. Secondly, not only is it a fundamentally different vision than that supplied by conservatism, but insofar as it is another version of Rationalism, neoconservatism and conservatism are mutually antagonistic.

Chapter 2

CONSERVATISM vs. NEOCONSERVATISM: RELIGION AND IDEOLOGY

IN 1956, THE English philosopher Michael Oakeshott published "On Being Conservative," [78] a statement of "the conservative disposition" as he conceived it. Although largely well received, Oakeshott's conception of conservatism was not without its critics. Among their number was the American intellectual and self-avowed "conservative" Irving Kristol who, while admitting to "loving every line" of Oakeshott's essay, of admiring it "immensely," claimed that its "irredeemably secular" character repelled him.[79] Oakeshott's vision of conservatism, he charged, is insufficiently religious in two respects.

First, Kristol imputes to it an obsession with *the present* that must be anathema to Jewish and Christian sensibilities by reason of its neglect of the past and the future. Jews and Christians can't but find that "it is impossible...to have the kinds of attitudes toward the past and the future that Oakeshott's conservative disposition celebrates," for their traditions "link us to the past and to the future with an intensity lacking in Oakeshott's vision." [80]

Secondly, the centrality of place that Oakeshott allegedly

assigns to the present not only renders it unpalatable to *traditional* religion; it violates as well the spirit of *the civic religion of America*. Americans, Kristol explains, have an "emphatic and explicit" commitment to their past that is "ideological;" [81] theirs is an "ideological patriotism" that is rooted in the United States' identity as "a 'creedal' nation," a nation to which anyone can belong irrespective of "ethnicity, or blood ties of any kind, or lineage, or length of residence even...." The uniquely "ideological" character of American patriotism and the foundational "creed" from which it springs, Kristol contends, are both "suffused with a kind of religious sensibility" that constitutes what can legitimately be called a "civic religion." [82]

Although there are indeed "tensions" between "American religiosity and the more secular 'civic religion,'" among the several critical respects in which they coincide is that they "both are, in general, future-oriented and 'progressive' in their political vision." [83]

In examining Oakeshott's characterization of "the conservative disposition," I will show that Kristol's two prong "religious critique" of it reflects a fundamental misconception of both classical Christianity as well as the classical conservatism to which Oakeshott gives expression. This misconception on Kristol's part is in turn a function of the fact that the *neoconservatism* to which Kristol subscribes is not, in fact, a form of conservatism at all.

II

In the essay under discussion, Oakeshott insists upon a distinction between, on the one hand, a "conservative disposition" *per se* and, on the other, such a disposition *in politics*. So crucial to his analysis is this distinction that, without it, Oakeshott's understanding of conservatism readily collapses into something else of another kind, another variety of conservatism, perhaps, but one of a comprehensive character that he expressly repudiates. Kristol, though, fails to (at least explicitly) address this distinction. In order to refute his "religious critique," we shall look first at Oakeshott's exposition of a generally conservative disposition. In the next section we will focus on his examination of this disposition in politics.

From the outset of his essay, Oakeshott is clear that his concern is not with "a creed or a doctrine, but a disposition." He writes: "To be conservative is to be disposed to think and behave in certain manners," and "to prefer certain kinds of conduct and certain conditions of human circumstances to others...." One who is conservative, Oakeshott continues, "is...disposed to make certain kinds of choices." [84] The conservative "prefer[s] the familiar to the unknown...the tried to the untried, fact to mystery, the actual to the possible, the limited to the unbounded, the near to the distant, the sufficient to the superabundant, the convenient to the perfect, present laughter to utopian bliss."

The conservative's preferences constitute "a propensity to use and enjoy what is available rather than to wish for or to look for something else," "to delight in what is present rather than what was or what may be." [85] The conservative temperament is partial to the present.

It is this attachment to what is present that Kristol deems incompatible with Judaism and Christianity. However, that Oakeshott's account of conservatism, with its present-mindedness, is in keeping with an enduring reading of the Christian tradition should become evident once we grasp that it is motivated, first and foremost, by an aversion, not just to change as such, but to *the rapid* change characteristic of contemporary Western societies, a phenomenon simultaneously driven by and reflective of *greed* and the penchant to *exploit*. Westerners have a "lust for change" that renders all "pieties fleeting" and "loyalties" "evanescent" as "the eye is ever on the new model." The problem is that "we are acquisitive to the point of greed," Oakeshott tells us, "ready to drop the bone we have for its reflection magnified in the mirror of the future." [86]

This restlessness with the present and the exclusive focus on the future by which it's accompanied stand in glaring contrast to the conservative's preference "to use and enjoy what is available" here and now "rather than to wish for or to look for something else," to opt for "present laughter" over "utopian bliss." [87] Changes "are without effect only upon those who notice nothing," and they "can be welcomed indiscriminately only by those…who are strangers to love and affection," for change, inescapably involving as it does the loss of something to which we've become attached, is "an emblem of extinction," an unmistakable "threat to identity…." [88]

It is not for nothing, Oakeshott reminds us, that "heaven is the dream of a changeless no less than a perfect world." [89] The conservative disposition, though, "breeds attachment and affection;" [90] the conservative's is "a disposition to enjoy rather than exploit." [91]

Inasmuch as they value it for the substantive satisfactions it is expected to yield, those who are preoccupied with the future—those of a "progressive" orientation—impose upon all human relationships and activities an "utilitarian" character. [92] Yet there are relationships and activities like friendship, patriotism, and conversation that are resolutely *not* utilitarian but, rather, "dramatic;" in such contexts, the conservative disposition—present-mindedness—is singularly apt.

For instance, while it is perfectly proper to continually change butchers until you find one that provides you with the service that you want, "to discard friends because they do not behave as we expected and refuse to be educated to our requirements is the conduct of a man who has altogether mistaken the character of friendship." [93] The value of friendship doesn't derive from any future benefits or rewards that it may produce, for the essence of friendship consists in "familiarity, not usefulness [.]"

Religion, at least as it is construed within the Jewish and

Christian traditions, is not unlike friendship, patriotism, and conversation in that it too "demands a conservative disposition as a condition of its enjoyment." [94] Contrary to Kristol's contention, the emphasis on the present upon which Oakeshott's conception of conservatism pivots is not only *consonant with* those modes of religious thought that have historically informed the Western imagination; such modes *require* nothing less than the "dramatic" stance that *contentment*—as opposed to true *happiness* or *bliss*—with the present entail.

In his *Confessions,* Saint Augustine writes that people "attempt to grasp eternal things, but their heart flutters among the changing things of past and future [.]" [95] From at least the time that Augustine articulated his famed analysis of time, orthodox Christian thought marked a radical departure from paganism in interpreting eternality in terms, not of endless time, but God's *timelessness.* God's eternality or timelessness means that for God there is neither past nor future but a forever-abiding Present, for He transcends "all past times in the sublimity of an ever present eternity," as Augustine writes. "Your years are one day, and your day is not each day, but today," for with God "today is eternity." [96]

In contrast to eternity, "time is a kind of distention," [97] and since Augustine, like all human beings, is a temporally embodied being, he confesses to being scattered or "dissipated in many ways upon many things," "distracted amid times, whose order I do not know," and "torn asunder by tumult and change [.]" The goods for which human beings clamor—the goods among which they are *distended*—being temporal, are mutable and, hence, perishable. Inasmuch as our lives are marked by an insatiable striving for one satisfaction after another, satisfactions that, if they can be obtained at all, can be realized only at some future time, we never live in the present, but are scattered among times. Augustine prays for release from this flux that threatens to rip him into pieces so that he will no longer be "distended but extended, *not to things that shall be and shall pass away*, but 'to those things which are before'" and "which neither come nor go." [98]

The "present" with which Oakeshott expresses concern in his description of the conservative disposition is admittedly *temporal*, not *eternal*. Yet there can be no denying that from the Christian perspective, as preeminently illustrated by Augustine, that both fasten attention upon what *is* as opposed to either what *was* or what *may be* establishes that the temporal present and the eternal present are not only not unrelated; the former is the only phase of temporality that supplies the link between time and eternity. The satisfaction that people derive from friendship and conversation, patriotism and prayer, being *intrinsic* to those activities, demands a present-mindedness that, however imperfectly and incompletely, arrests their restlessness, their "distention" over "things that shall be and shall pass away." In acquiring an appreciation for the present just because it is present, we succeed to some measure in abating the paralysis that springs from both those anxieties concerning an uncertain future as well as those arising from a determined past. The orientation toward the present for which Oakeshott's account of conservatism calls, in conveying intimations of eternity, is an approximation of it.

This is the insight that the Christian tradition has affirmed. In the seventeenth century, the French Catholic thinker Blaise Pascal expressed it well. He laments both the folly that leads us to "wander about in times that do not belong to us," while failing to "think of the only one that does," as well as the vanity that propels us to "dream of times that are not and blindly flee the only one that is." The fact is that while "we recall the past" and "anticipate the future," "we never keep to the present." Pascal says that "we try to give" the present "the support of the future, and think of how we are going to arrange things over which we have no control for a time we can never be sure of reaching." The only time we think of the present is when we are interested in determining "what light it throws on our plans for the future." In short:

> *The present is never our end. The past and the present are our means, the future alone our end. Thus we never actually live, but hope to live, and since we are always planning on how to be happy, it is inevitable that we should never be so.*[99]

Oakeshott's vision of conservatism, then, far from being inconsistent with traditional religion, is entirely in keeping with it. From the Christian perspective, the self is always in danger of being dissolved, for it is "distended" among things, among times. Oakeshott's conservatism draws upon a resource—focus on the present—to abate the flux. Admittedly, the temporal present is a shadowy and remote image of the Eternal Presence in which all hopes will finally rest. Still, the enjoyment of the present anticipates, even if only faintly, nothing less than *beatitude,* the bliss experienced in the immediate encounter with God to which all Christians aspire.

III

According to Kristol, Oakeshott's statement of conservatism is unpalatable not only to Jews and Christians, but to *Americans,* for it stands in irreconcilable conflict with America's "civic religion," its "creed." Prior to unpacking this latter notion, we must first attend to Oakeshott's position on the relationship between conservatism and *politics,* for Kristol's charge here is that Oakeshott's vision of conservatism is politically unfeasible for America.

Oakeshott is adamant that (what we may, for convenience's sake, call) "political conservatism" is logically separable from all of those metaphysical, moral, or religious ideas—like God, "natural law," "an 'organic' theory of human society," and "the absolute value of human personality," to name but a few[100]—upon which it has traditionally been thought to depend. He bluntly states that "a disposition to be conservative in politics does not entail either that we should" hold any of these ideas "to be true or even that we should suppose them to be true." Rather, a disposition to be conservative in politics "is tied to…certain beliefs about the activity of governing and the instruments of government, and it is in terms of" these beliefs *alone* "that it can be made to appear intelligible." [101] What are these beliefs?

Oakeshott's reply is to the point: it is the belief, coupled with "the observation of our current manner of living"—a manner of living of which individuality and plurality are the most salient features—that "governing is a specific and limited activity" of providing "general rules of conduct" for the sake, not of "imposing substantive activities," but of "enabling people to pursue the activities of their own choice with minimum frustration [.]" [102] And what this means is that "the office of government is not to impose other beliefs and activities upon its subjects;" it is "not to tutor or to educate them," "to make them better or happier,"; government is not "to direct" citizens or "to galvanize them into action, to lead them or to co-ordinate their activities so that no occasion of conflict shall occur [.]" Government is "merely to rule," an office that, being "a specific and limited activity" and, thus, "easily corrupted when it is combined with any other," can't afford to suffer dilution.[103]

A disposition to be conservative in politics, then, demands an aversion, not just to change, but change of a certain type, what Oakeshott calls "innovation"—those changes that are the products of deliberate design. In addition to the most basic consideration that, like all change, the "improvements" sought by the innovator—if and when, in fact, they truly *are* improvements—are accompanied by loss, the conservative's reluctance to embrace innovation stems from his rejection of the belief that "unless great changes are afoot," there is "nothing happening [.]" It isn't dreams of an unbounded future that engage him but, rather, "the use and enjoyment of things as they are [.]"[104]

Yet the conservative's reticence regarding change and innovation shouldn't be confused with a doctrine or creed. The conservative is well aware both that change is a fundamental, inescapable fact of life and that innovation is necessary and desirable in some instances. Still, he prefers changes of one sort to those of another.

The conservative thinks that the proposed innovation should approximate as closely as possible "growth:" it should be "intimated in and not merely imposed upon the situation." Moreover, the change in question should be "a response to some specific defect" rather than aimed at realizing some "generally improved condition of human circumstances." Finally, it should be "small and limited," not "large and indefinite," and should proceed at a "slow rather than rapid pace [.]"[105]

Now, we may ask, how does this idea of politics, with its assignation to government of the modest (yet indispensable) role of maintaining order and its aversion to change and innovation, conflict with America's creed, as Kristol charges?

It is crucial to recognize that when Kristol and others refer to the United States as a creedal nation, they follow the lead of Abraham Lincoln who famously said of America that it is "dedicated" to a "proposition," the proposition that "all men are created equal." Because America is a "creedal" or "propositional" nation, all that American patriotism requires is an affirmation of this *principle* of equality that is purportedly at the core of the American founding: the particularities of race and ethnicity that had historically defined all other patriotisms are irrelevant to it. It also accounts for why Kristol couldn't but find the temporal thrust of Oakeshott's conservatism unacceptable, for the logic of the egalitarianism with which he identifies America's creed is "future-oriented and 'progressive'" politically.[106]

A creed or ideology is a proposition or set of related propositions to which anyone, in theory, can subscribe, and the American creed that Kristol affirms, a doctrine of "natural rights" expressing a "principle of equality" that is embodied in the Declaration of Independence, has unabashedly universalistic pretensions. In Kristol's judgment, Americans don't affirm only *their* "unalienable" rights, but the inalienable, God-derived rights of all of humanity. In proclaiming these rights to be "self-evident" truths, the Declaration construes them as principles of Reason, principles, that is, that are accessible to all people in all places and at all times. This in turn implies that in addition to being universalistic, the idea of a "creedal" or "ideological" nation is as well *rationalistic:* for Kristol and his ilk, one's identity as an American is established by nothing more than an intellectual exercise whereby one rationally assents to the propositions encapsulated in the Declaration. Given this unqualified quasi-religious commitment to "the Rights of Man," America must forever be future-oriented, for as long as human rights are threatened, and regardless of *where* they are imperiled, her work in the world will never be complete.

It is *this*, I contend, to which Kristol's opposition to Oakeshott's account of conservatism ultimately boils down: it is isn't the latter's alleged incompatibility with traditional religion that motivates it but, rather, its undeniable incompatibility with the rationalistic and universalistic character of the ideology of "natural" or "human rights" with which Kristol equates America's "civic religion" and of which, not coincidentally, his understanding of "conservatism"—what is now called "neoconservatism"—is a resounding affirmation.

That it is Kristol's subscription to this species of Enlightenment liberal rationalism that fundamentally informs his distaste for Oakeshott's statement of conservatism is beyond mere speculation as Kristol himself acknowledges it. In "looking back over the past forty years," Kristol writes, he realizes that his distaste for Oakeshott's analysis of the conservative disposition stemmed from the fact that Kristol "was then in the earliest stages of intellectual pregnancy with those attitudes and dispositions that later emerged as 'neoconservatism,'" an American political philosophical orientation "very different from the kind of ideal English conservatism that Oakeshott was celebrating so brilliantly." [107]

As Oakeshott understands it, the conservative disposition is essentially a disposition toward *change,* specifically, the *lust* for change that had come to dominate modern Western societies. In this respect, it is neither uniquely nor even distinctively English, much less ideally English. I have already shown this by locating it within the context of the Christian tradition and connecting it with thinkers as far removed from twentieth century England as Saint Augustine and Pascal. And whereas the English flavor of his articulation of *political* conservatism is indeed unmistakable, it is but a variant of the dominant understanding of classical conservatism since it first assumed a recognizably distinct shape in the words of Burke, widely regarded as "the patron saint" of modern conservatism.

Burke's philosophy was born of exactly the same impulse that animates Oakeshott's: an animus toward, in Oakeshott's words, a "lust for change," that is, *radical* change and innovation. As Burke writes, "A spirit of innovation is generally the result of a selfish temper and confined views," [108] and "the spirit of change" that innovators encourage consists of "signals" for "revolutions" that are informed by "the total contempt which prevails" among innovators and revolutionaries for "all ancient institutions" [109]

Burke cautions against indulging that "unprincipled facility of changing the state as often and as much and in as many ways as there are floating fancies or fashions" [110] and implores the innovators to exercise "due caution" when attending to problems by eschewing the fantasy that "reformation" of the state can consist in its "subversion." [111] With innovators "it is a sufficient motive to destroy an old scheme of things, because it is an old one," but as for what they erect in its place, "they are in no sort of fear with regard to the duration of a building run up in haste."

The duration of institutions and of whole governments, Burke continues, is of no interest to innovators "who think little or nothing has been done before their time, and who place all their hopes" in future "discoveries;" they sorely lack a "principle of attachment...." [112] Innovators "see no merit or demerit in any man, or any action, or any political principle, any further than as they may forward or retard their design of change," [113] a design that must appear as "a great change of scene," "a magnificent stage effect," "a grand spectacle to rouse the imagination." [114] With their abstract metaphysics of "the Rights of Man," [115] a "mechanic philosophy" that promises to preclude "our institutions" from ever becoming "embodied" in human hearts, from eliciting "love, veneration, admiration, or attachment," [116] innovators are filled with a "vanity, restlessness, petulance, and a spirit of intrigue...." [117]

Notice, Oakeshott in resolutely eschewing the abstract, rationalistic ontological presuppositions underwriting the "lust for change" informing "the progressive" or future-centered orientation of "the innovator," is merely improvising on just those themes to which Burke first gave expression nearly 200 years earlier. To put this point more straightforwardly, since Burke set the tone for subsequent conservative thinkers, and since Oakeshott has made this tone his own, the position that he delineates and for which he supplies an apology, far from being a deviation from historical conservatism, is a faithful adaptation of it. This in turn implies that Kristol, in rejecting Oakeshott's understanding of conservatism and deeming it irreconcilable with America's "civic religion," rejects *conservatism* and holds *it* to be incompatible with the American "creed."

It isn't America, however, with which conservatism (as construed either by Burke or Oakeshott) fails to cohere; it is Kristol's *neoconservatism* and its rationalistic *conception* of America that cannot be reconciled with it.

Of course, the idea that the essence of America is located in a creed, a set of propositions or principles specifying trans-cultural, trans-historical "rights" of which all human beings are said to be in possession is not uniquely held by neoconservatives; the opening lines of the Declaration of Independence—a defining American document—provided generations of Americans since our country's founding reason to endorse it, or at least something like it. Oakeshott, in fact, is among those to have observed this.

In another essay, "Rationalism in Politics," Oakeshott writes that the Declaration "is a characteristic product of the *saeculum rationalisticm"* and "one of the sacred documents of the politics of Rationalism" that, along with some others, were interpreted to justify not just the bloody French Revolution in response to which Burke gave form to conservatism, but "many later adventures in *the rationalist reconstruction of society"* [118] as well. He elaborates: "The early history of the United States of America is an instructive chapter in the history of the politics of Rationalism," for the unique circumstances of early America, including and especially the fact that it was populated by colonial subjects who saw themselves as taming a vast wilderness, made the latter "disposed to believe...that the proper organization of a society and the conduct of its affairs were based upon abstract principles, and not upon a tradition...." [119] The moral "principles" on the basis of which Americans believe their society is grounded are not thought to be "the product of civilization," but "natural, 'written in the whole volume of human nature,'" and "to be discovered in nature by human reason, by a technique of inquiry available alike to all men and requiring no extraordinary intelligence in its use." [120]

There are a few things to observe here. First, Oakeshott and Kristol are in at least partial agreement that the United States, as it is seen through the lens of the Declaration, lends itself to the rationalistic reading that both make of it, and on this score, their shared judgment is sound as far it goes.

Second, this evaluation only goes so far. It is true that America can, with some plausibility, be construed as a "creedal" or "propositional" nation; but at the same time, it can, with a much greater share of plausibility, be understood as an "historical" nation that, like any other, does indeed owe its existence to just those "accidents" that have conspired to form every other society that has ever existed but which an "ideological patriotism" precludes.

Although the Declaration is admittedly littered with universalistic rhetoric reflective of eighteenth century Enlightenment rationalism, the bulk of it, consisting as it does of numerous grievances issued by *English* subjects against their King in a shared idiom, is unmistakably historically particular. That the founding generation spearheaded what essentially amounted to an English secessionist movement is something that was widely understood on both sides of the Atlantic, and in England, while he urged his government to reconcile its differences with the American colonists, "the Father of modern conservatism" himself sympathized with the latter. Burke is quick to remind all that "the people of the colonies *are descendants of Englishmen.*" As such, they inherited England's characteristic "bias," *not* for some "abstract" concept of "liberty," but for *"liberty according to English ideas and on English principles."* In fact, even the principal grounds on which Americans declare their independence are a function of the distinctively English conception of liberty that they cherish, for unlike those conceptions that have dominated at different times and in different societies according to which monetary considerations played little or no role, "the great contests for freedom in this country [England]...were from the earliest times chiefly upon the question of taxes." [121] Burke informs "the British Colonists in North America" that they should not believe "that the whole, or even the uninfluenced majority, of Englishmen in this island are enemies to *their own blood* on the American continent," and that the English generally long "to continue united with you, in order that a people of *one origin* and *one character* should be directed to the rational objects of government by joint counsels...." [122]

Thirdly, although Oakeshott, in commenting on the rationalistic character of the Declaration, readily observes the pervasive propensity of Americans to believe that theirs is a "propositional" or "creedal" nation, he no less readily debunks this idea as a delusion: (at least some of) the early American colonists believed, and subsequent generations of Americans may continue to believe, that their society has been arranged in terms of abstract principles (or "the proposition" that "all men are created equal"), but, in fact, such principles are but abridgments of a centuries-old, culturally-specific practice. As Oakeshott explains, "the inspiration of Jefferson and the other founders of American independence," far from being universalistic "principles" or "propositions" accessible to all rational beings everywhere, was, rather, "the ideology which Locke had distilled from the English political tradition." [123] The principles and/or ideals affirmed in the Declaration are not unlike any others in being "a sediment" that, as such, "have significance only so long as they are suspended in a religious or social tradition, so long as they belong to a religious or social life." [124]

Thus, Oakeshott's understanding of political conservatism, though certainly in conflict with Kristol's neoconservatism and the supra-historical conception of America that it embraces, is not, ultimately, at odds with the historically-centered—and accurate—interpretation of America shared by Burke and (of all people!) the author of precisely that document, the Declaration, that gave rise to Kristol's rationalistic reading America as a "creedal" nation.

Conclusion

By now there should no longer be any doubts that Kristol's "religious critique" of Oakeshott's statement of "the conservative disposition" is both a function of the neoconservatism to which he subscribes as well as fundamentally misplaced: the present-mindedness that pervades Oakeshott's conservatism, whether it is oriented toward politics or any other aspect of life, coheres comfortably with traditional Christianity, and while it is definitely incompatible with America conceived as a *creedal* nation, such a conception is the product of a misreading that springs from a failure to contextualize the principles affirmed in the Declaration within the culturally and historically-specific English tradition from whence they were elicited. Oakeshott's articulation of conservatism is continuous with the conservative tradition to which Burke gave unprecedented expression two centuries earlier, and, as such, *is* compatible with America understood as an *historical* nation.

Chapter 3

CONSERVATISM v. NEOCONSERVATISM: PATRIOTISM

IS PATRIOTISM A virtue? Both conservatives and neoconservatives have answered this question in the affirmative. However, in what follows, I argue for two theses.

First, while conservatism endorses tradition-centered epistemological, metaphysical, and moral suppositions that lead to patriotism's being a virtue, the philosophical framework of neoconservatism—what I call "Rationalism-Universalism"—precludes this possibility.

Second, while conservatism rejects the Rational*ism* and Universal*ism* of their opponents in favor of an epistemology rooted in *tradition* and a morality of particularity, respectively, it does *not* reject rational*ity* and universal*ity* as such. Conservatism, I show, contains the conceptual resources for resolving the perennial "problem of universals" in a way that allows a place for *both* universality *and* particularity.

Given Burke's widely recognized prominence within the conservative intellectual tradition, and given that his *Reflections on the Revolution in France* is just as widely regarded as the paradigmatic statement of conservative thought, it is to the Burke of the *Reflections* that I here turn in unpacking the philosophical vision of conservatism. Moreover, the *Reflections*, to as great an extent as any other work, draws the contrasts between conservatism and the Rationalism-Universalism that it emerged to combat.

Since neoconservatives continue to command considerable influence over the formation of American foreign and domestic policy, and because some of these policies have been prescribed under the pretext of patriotism—usually called "American Exceptionalism"—I bring neoconservatism into focus by looking at some of its scholarly and *popular* proponents, from Leo Strauss and Allan Bloom to Charles Krauthammer and William J. Bennett.

This paper consists of four sections. In the first, I analyze patriotism, Rationalism, and Universalism. In the second and third sections, I explore neoconservatism and conservatism, respectively. The fourth section consists in using conservatism as a means toward resolving the problem of the universal and the particular.

Patriotism, Rationalism & Universalism

Philosopher Andrew Oldenquist explains that patriotism, being loyalty to one's country, has (until recently) received scarce attention from contemporary philosophers because philosophers "generally neglect to discuss loyalties at all." [125]

Loyalty is always loyalty to a particular *this* or *that* and, as such, demands an attitude of *partiality*. In stark contrast, the Universalism embodied by the prevailing moral vision of modern philosophy, underwritten as it is by the epistemology of Rationalism, requires *impartiality*. Thus, contemporary ethics has generally allowed, *at best*, a subordinate place for the concrete and particular vis-à-vis the moral life: partiality toward the particular is treated as either non-moral or even immoral.

The Rationalism to which I here refer is what elsewhere has been described variously as "constructivism," [126] "Gnosticism," [127] "Logicism," [128] etc. Its proponents conceive human rationality in abstraction from the countless culturally and historically-specific contingencies, the traditions, that shape it. This being so, thinkers like Descartes, Spinoza, and Leibniz—philosophers who have long been recognized as rationalists—are indeed proponents of Rationalism, but so too are such "empiricists" as John Locke, Jeremy Bentham, John S. Mill, and others who construe "experience" solely in terms of the "sensations" and "reflections" [129] of what appears to *the individual*. From the Rationalist's perspective, the "general bank and capital of nations and of ages," [130] the wisdom of generations, in terms of which Burke defined experience, counts for little or nothing. In fact, it is often held in low regard, as something from which the intellect needs to be emancipated.

In his exposition of Rationalism, Michael Oakeshott notes that while all cognition consists of two types, "technical" and "practical" or "traditional," Rationalists err in acknowledging only the former as genuine knowledge. Technical knowledge consists of "rules" that, because they "may be, deliberately learned, remembered, and, as we say, put into practice," are susceptible of "precise formulation [.]" Practical or traditional knowledge, however, defies express excogitation, for it "exists only in use, is not reflective and (unlike technique) cannot be formulated in rules." It can be imparted, but "the method" by which it is disseminated "is not the method of formulated doctrine." [131]

That which can be stated clearly in speech and boiled down into a set of propositions that, in theory, anyone at any time and in any place can access, appeals to the Rationalist mind because of the impression of "certainty" [132] that it conveys. Familiarity with thinkers as disparate as Descartes the rationalist and Locke "the empiricist" reveals that the "tabula rasa" of the latter no less than the methodological skepticism of the former reflect the attraction of both to the idea that technical knowledge "seems to be a self-complete sort of knowledge," one that "seems to range between an identifiable initial point (where it breaks in upon sheer ignorance) and an identifiable terminal point, where it is complete, as in learning the rules of a game." Also, "the application" of technical knowledge appears, "as nearly as possible, purely mechanical," and its proponents suppose that it relies on nothing "not itself provided in the technique." [133] That the knowledge of a technique or method is always nothing more or less than the distillation of a practice or tradition, the *product* of a pre-reflective, customary or habitual manner of life, is lost upon the Rationalist.

The Universalism of Rationalists is inseparable from their epistemology. Given that all knowledge is obtained by way of rules or principles—propositions—that are (potentially) accessible to *everyone,* regardless of time or place, moral knowledge is achieved this way. What this means is that Rationalists think of moral knowledge in terms that are just as abstract and universal as the principles and rules by which all other knowledge is secured. So, the ontology—the stuff—of morality is, then, comprised primarily of *principles* and *ideals,* entities that, one way or another, reveal themselves to all minds. These abstractions are fundamental: They exist or subsist in advance of all human traditions and practices.

It is the epistemology of Rationalism and the ontological and ethical suppositions of Universalism that account for why ethicists have neglected loyalties. And it is this philosophical worldview that accounts for why, *when* they *have addressed* loyalty to one's country—patriotism—they have been disposed to view it as, not a virtue, but a *vice.*

David McCabe explicitly states that "liberal morality" [Rationalist-Universalism] is "fundamentally at odds" with patriotism, for the latter "may help tempt people away from the appropriate claims of equal moral treatment and towards something resembling group egoism." [134] Paul Gomberg is even more unabashed on this score in remarking that "on the most plausible assumptions about our world, patriotism is no better than racism." After all, "moral universalism implies that actions are to be governed by principles that give equal consideration to all people who might be affected by an action." [135] But patriotism is "a preference for one's fellow nationals or for one's own traditions and institutions over those of others," [136] and this in turn sounds dangerously like "ethnic and national chauvinism." [137]

Alasdair MacIntyre, a Catholic philosopher of the Aristotelian-Thomist persuasion and a proponent of patriotism makes the point. He observes that insofar as the patriot has "a peculiar regard...for the particular characteristics and merits and achievements of" his nation because they are *his* nation, [138] "the particularity" of the patriot's relationship to his country is "essential and ineliminable." [139] The patriot's morality is "a morality of particularist ties and solidarities," [140] of "a class of loyalty-exhibiting virtues" like "marital fidelity, the love of one's own family and kin, friendship, and loyalty to such institutions as schools and cricket or baseball clubs." [141] The morality of patriotism demands of the patriot "a peculiar devotion" to his country. It demands that he "regard such contingent social facts as where I was born and what government ruled over that place at that time, who my parents were, who my great-great-grandparents were, and so on, as deciding for me the question of what virtuous action is [.]"

Considering that the morality of the Rationalist-Universalist—what MacIntyre calls "liberal morality"—demands that moral agents abstract "from all social particularity and partiality" in rendering "impersonal" judgments, it is not only "systematically incompatible" [142] with viewing patriotism as a virtue; it actually "requires that patriotism—at least in any substantial version—be treated as a vice." [143]

As we will now see, despite their affirmations of patriotism, neoconservatives, being Rationalist-Universalists, logically have no option but to regard loyalty to one's country—patriotism—as a vice. Perhaps this accounts for why they tend to equate patriotism with what they call "American

Exceptionalism," a doctrine that demands devotion, not to a concrete, particular country, but to an abstract, universal set of principles or values.

Neoconservatism

In *Neoconservatism: Why We Need It*, Douglas Murray concedes that the philosopher Leo Strauss is both "a useful and necessary point of entry for any investigation of neoconservatism." [144] Indeed he is, for Strauss articulated an eloquent defense of the morality of natural rights that at once embodies the Rationalist-Universalism of the neoconservative vision.

In *Natural Right and History,* Strauss equates the rejection of natural right with "saying that all right is positive right," that what is just is what human beings—specifically "the legislators and the courts of the various countries" [145]—say is so. The rejection of natural right, he continues, "is identical with nihilism." [146] Among the "historicist" foes of "natural right" that he identifies are such "eminent conservatives" [147] as Edmund Burke. Burke and other conservatives came into their own while responding to "the natural rights doctrines that had prepared" the "cataclysm" of the French Revolution. They seemed "to have realized somehow," what Strauss himself realizes, "that the acceptance of any universal or abstract principles has necessarily a revolutionary, disturbing" and "unsettling effect [.]" [148]

Allan Bloom, one of Strauss's pupils, brings this philosophical vision to bear upon the American scene generally, and the topic of American patriotism, specifically, in his *The Closing of the American Mind,* a much celebrated work among neoconservatives. America, Bloom writes, "is one of the highest and most extreme achievements of the rational quest for the good life according to nature," for "its political structure" relies upon "the use of the rational principles of natural right [.]" [149] This means that "patriotism" must undergo a transformation. Whereas traditional societies instilled in its members "an instinctive, unqualified, even fanatic patriotism," education in the United States has been geared toward inspiring in its citizens a "reflected, rational, calm, even self-interested loyalty [.]" Yet this loyalty is not to the country as such, but to its "form of government and its rational principles [.]" From this moral perspective, "Class, race, religion, national origin or culture all disappear or become dim when bathed in the light of natural rights, which give men common interests and make them truly brothers." [150]

Notice, from this vantage point, it is abstract principles and *"the form"* of government that exists in America that become proper objects of the patriot's devotion. This form of government is the "Enlightenment" *ideal* of "liberal democracy." "There is practically no contemporary regime that is not somehow a result of Enlightenment, and the best of modern regimes—liberal democracy—is entirely its product." Liberal democracy is "the regime of equality and liberty, of the rights of man," and "the regime of reason," [151] and America is its epitome in that it is the first country in all of human history to have been founded upon "rational principles."

This conception of morality and the requirements of American patriotism now inform "the conservative movement," i.e. neoconservatism.

Douglas Murray, for example, establishes his commitment to neoconservative morality when he commends Ronald Reagan for his "evil empire" speech. Reagan was a neoconservative president because he argued "for the encouragement and kindling of democracy across the globe." [152]

Murray is under no illusions regarding the relationship between neoconservatism and conservatism: the former differs "socially, economically, and philosophically" from the latter. More to the point, neoconservatives represent "revolutionary conservatism," [153] for their prime objective of "erasing tyrannies and spreading democracy" require "interventionism, nation-building, and many of the other difficulties that had long concerned traditional conservatives."[154]

Irving Kristol is "the godfather" of neoconservatism. Neoconservatives, he writes, accept "the equality of natural rights" enshrined in the Declaration of Independence[155] and view them as "the principles of" America's "establishment,"[156] the principles of "the universal creed" upon which the nation is "based."[157] The United States, then, is "a creedal nation"[158] with a "'civilizing mission'"[159] to promote "American values"[160] throughout the world, to see to it "that other governments respect our conception of individual rights as the foundation of a just regime and a good society." Kristol is unambiguous in his profession of the American faith: the United States, given its status as a "great power" and its "ideological" nature, does indeed have a responsibility "in those places and at those times where conditions permit" it "to flourish" to "'make the world safe for democracy."[161]

That the neoconservative's Rationalist-Universalism is *the* moral vision of the contemporary "conservative movement" is gotten easily enough. Take, for instance, nationally syndicated radio talk show host William Bennett. In previous times, Bennett claims, children in this country were educated to appreciate "the superior goodness of the American way of life,"[162] and they learned that American patriotism consisted of "our steadfast devotion to the ideals of freedom and equality." American patriots, beginning with "the patriots of 1776 and 1787," have always been devoted "to something quite new—a new nation conceived in a new way and dedicated to a self-evident truth that all men are created equal," "a country tied together in loyalty to a principle [.]"[163]

Fox News celebrity and nationally syndicated columnist Charles Krauthammer locates himself unmistakably within this neoconservative intellectual tradition in describing America as "a nation uniquely built not on blood, race or consanguinity, but on *a proposition*"—the proposition that all human beings are created equal, or possess equal rights. Krauthammer, along with his fellow neoconservatives, refers to this creed as

"American exceptionalism." From it, he makes the characteristically neoconservative move and deduces a "value-driven foreign policy"—what he calls "democratic globalism." From the latter vantage point, "the engine of history" is "not the will to power but the will to freedom" [164]—i.e. "the spread of democracy" around the planet.[165] Krauthammer asserts that "America's national interest" is "an expression of values." [166]

The vast majority of Krauthammer's colleagues among the "conservative" punditry class agree with him on all of these points. Nationally syndicated columnist and radio show host Dennis Prager, for instance, affirms "American exceptionalism" while explaining that it is nothing more or less than the belief that "America often knows better than the world what is right and wrong." And why is this? For the most part, belief in "American exceptionalism" rises from the "Judeo-Christian" character of America's "values." [167] Though these "values" have going for them their "moral superiority" to all others, they are also of "universal applicability" and "eminently exportable." Prager is unabashed: "These magnificent American values are applicable to virtually every society in the world." [168]

That neoconservatives construe morality in terms of abstract universal principles and/or ideals that are "self-evident"—that subsist prior to and independently of all traditions—establishes their commitment to Rationalist-Universalist morality. And that, in keeping with this commitment, they identify patriotism with loyalty to these very principles and ideals means that neoconservatives have no logical option but to regard patriotism, as traditionally conceived, as morally noxious. After all, as Bloom said, devotion to such particularities as "class, race, religion, national origin or culture" comprises a "fanatic patriotism," i.e. a morally unacceptable patriotism. Such contingencies of time and place "disappear or become dim when bathed in the light of natural rights," for the latter pertain to *everyone*.

There can be no place for devotion to one's country in

the neoconservatives' philosophical schema. However, as we shall now see, by the lights of the conservative vision articulated by Burke, patriotism must be a virtue.

Conservatism

The Rationalism and Universalism of his foes among the French Revolutionaries Burke eviscerated as a "barbarous" [169] and a "mechanic philosophy" that "banishes the affections [.]" [170] Strauss convicted Burke for promoting a "depreciation of reason." He was mistaken. Burke's rejection of the Rationalist's conception of Reason is no more tantamount to a rejection of reason itself than the rejection of scient*ism,* say, is tantamount to a rejection of science. Burke valued reason, but he realized that, as an individual standard of judgment, it becomes a private conceit unless it takes into account the civilization in which it operates and the vital role of tradition and prejudice, understood as the inculcation of moral sentiment, for advancing the collective social Good. The unencumbered Intellect of Rationalists is a dreamy fiction— "delusive plausibilities" [171] and "mazes of metaphysic sophistry" [172]—that promises nightmarish results.

The epistemology of the conservative, on the other hand, is grounded in tradition. "We are afraid to put men to live and trade each on his own private stock of reason," Burke famously states, for "we suspect that the stock in each man is small, and that the individual would do better to avail himself of the general bank and capital of nations and of ages." He then draws his audience's attention to what he perceives to be the fundamental difference between the conservative conception of knowledge on behalf of which he argues and that of the Rationalist conception that he rejects. "Many of our men of speculation," Burke asserts, "instead of exploding general prejudices, employ their sagacity to discover the latent wisdom which prevails in them." [173] Rather than "cast away the coat of prejudice" in favor of "the naked reason," the wise retain the prejudice, for it alone supplies a "motive to give action to that reason, and an affection which will give it permanence." [174]

While Rationalists view Reason as an arbiter of tradition, the conservative holds that reason, shaped as it is by tradition, develops in tandem with the latter. Notice, much knowledge is what Oakeshott calls "practical knowledge," knowledge that is in important respects *inarticulate*, the fruits of the experiences of generations spanning centuries and millennia. Furthermore, because this knowledge is passed on from "those who are dead" to "those who are living" and "those who are to be born," [175] it takes the form of *tradition*. So, contrary to what Rationalists imply, reason can no more discard tradition without discarding itself than can language do the same.

The Rationalist-Universalist equates morally right conduct with subscription to abstract principles and ideals. The Universalism of Burke's rivals assumed the form of "natural rights," rights that are supposed to subsist prior to and independently of culture and civilization. The problem, as Burke saw it, with "'the rights of men'" is that they "admit of no temperament and no compromise: anything withheld from their full demand is so much of fraud and injustice." When governments and societies are brought before the tribunal of ostensibly universal principles like those specifying "natural rights," "an old and beneficent government," no less than "the most violent tyranny or the greenest usurpation," [176] is susceptible of condemnation. The reason for this is simple enough: the "abstract perfection" of these principles is their "practical defect." Doctrines of "the rights of men," insofar as they impute to men "a right to everything," make them "want everything." [177]

The morality of the conservative, in contrast, is tradition-specific, located in the interstices of the concrete relationships, the contingencies of time and place that inform the individual's identity and give texture to his moral vision. It is not to abstract universal principles, but to the local, the particular relationships, "the subdivision," "the little platoon" to which "we belong in society" that allegiance is due.

And it is precisely because the first, most basic, and most enduring of all "little platoons" is *the family* that Burke calls upon this imagery when characterizing the relationship between the individual and his country: love of country—patriotism—he argues, is analogous to love of family.

The English, Burke writes, "derive all we possess as *an inheritance from our forefathers.*" The English Constitution constitutes "a sort of family settlement, grasped as in a kind of mortmain forever." Burke regards "our liberties as an *entailed inheritance* derived to us from our forefathers, and to be transmitted to our posterity—as an estate specially belonging to the people of this kingdom, without any reference whatever to any other more general or prior right." Appeals to the latter Burke rejects as both unnecessary and undesirable. He and his compatriots are the inheritors of "privileges, franchises, and liberties from a long line of ancestors." [178]

Because familial relations are the products of nature, not artifice or convention, by casting national ties in these terms patriots can claim to "receive," "hold," and "transmit" their "government" and "privileges" similarly to the ways in which they "enjoy and transmit" their "property and…lives." [179] Burke explains:

> In this choice of inheritance we have given to our frame of polity the image of a relation in blood: binding up the Constitution of our country with our dearest domestic ties; adopting our fundamental laws into the bosom of our family affections; keeping inseparable, and cherishing with the warmth of all their combined and mutually reflected charities, our state, our hearths, our sepulchres, and our altars. [180]

In addition to the fact that it "furnishes a sure principle of conservation, and a sure principle of transmission, without at all excluding a principle of improvement," [181] the idea of an inheritance inspires us to always act "as if in the presence of canonized forefathers [.]" [182]

Thus, unlike Rationalist-Universalists who are always on the move to revolutionize society so as to make it comport with their abstract designs, conservatives have "a sullen resistance to innovation" reflective of their belief that "we still bear the stamp of our forefathers." [183] It's the idea of an inheritance that guarantees that "no man should approach to look into" the "defects or corruptions" of his society "but with due caution," as he would attend "to the wounds of a father with pious awe and trembling solicitude." It with "horror" that patriots look upon those Rationalist-Universalists who are like "children" in being "prompt" to "rashly to hack that aged parent [their country] in pieces and put him into the kettle of magicians" where, they imagine, with "their poisonous weeds and wild incantations," they will be able to "regenerate the paternal constitution and renovate their father's life." [184]

Genuine patriotism is loyalty to, not a universal principle, but a concrete, particular entity: one's country. For Burke, as for the generations of conservatives that he inspired, patriotism is, and can only be, a virtue for the same reason that loyalty to one's family is, and can only be, a virtue.

Yet this emphasis on moral particularity should not be taken to imply that Burke's conservatism excludes a role for universality. It is to the proposed resolution in Burke's thought of the perennial "problem of universals" that we now turn.

The Universal and the Particular

Western philosophy itself originated in the preoccupation of the first philosophers with resolving the relationship between the universal and the particular, the One and the many, the immutable and the mutable. The quest for a resolution continues. Neoconservatives, as I have argued, resolve the "problem of universals" by subordinating the particular—the particularities of tradition—to the universal, which, in turn, they identify with abstract principles, values, and ideals. Claes Ryn, a Burke admirer and veteran scholar who has spent decades endeavoring to simultaneously refute the Universalism of the neoconservative while achieving a synthesis of universality and particularity refers to neoconservatism's abstractions as "ahistorical notions of good." [185]

As we saw, Burke too rejects Universal*ism*. But this no more means that he rejected moral universal*ity* than the fact that he rejects Rational*ism* means that he rejected rational*ity*. Burke, rather, held that the development and exercise of the intellect and the consciousness of universal moral truths depend upon tradition. Burke, in other words, is among those who chose to resolve the problem of universals by seeking to *reconcile* both universality *and* particularity. Though Burke isn't always all that clear, I will argue for a position that I submit is consonant with the thrust and substance of Burke's reasoning.

In the *Reflections,* Burke writes that it is "the subdivision"—those forms of local association, "the little platoons" of family, friends, neighborhoods, towns, etc., into which we are born and educated—that is "the first principle (the germ, as it were) of public affections" and "the first link in the series by which we proceed towards a love to our country and to *mankind*." [186] Here, Burke reveals an awareness of a universal imperative to love universally. Thus, in one stroke he affirms the moral significance of both particularity and universality. However, two questions, the one epistemological, the other metaphysical, immediately pose themselves: *How* do we come by the knowledge that we have obligations to "mankind?" *What* is this universal of which we have knowledge? Though conceptually distinct, in practice, it is impossible to answer questions of the first type without simultaneously answering questions of the second.

Thomas Aquinas provides some assistance in helping to understand how, on my reading of him, Burke can claim that we possess knowledge of the universal. The Saint distinguishes two respects in which a statement can be "self-evident." Some propositions, he said, are self-evident in themselves, but *not to us*. Others are self-evident both in themselves and to us. If a person lacks the requisite familiarity with the relevant concepts or the philosophical reasoning needed to discern the logical implications of those concepts, then while the proposition in question—like the proposition, "God exists"—is self-evident per se, it will not be self-evident to that person. Thus, in order to acquire knowledge of God's existence, Aquinas thought that it was necessary that we reason backwards to the latter from what *is* self-evident *to us*: the world in which we find ourselves.[187] And this, in turn, we know through *experience*. Burke, I suggest, thinks similarly in regard to moral knowledge. There are, however, three important respects in which he differs from Aquinas's position on knowledge of God.

First, Aquinas, affirming a fundamental, ineradicable distinction between the objects of experience and God, uses the former to argue to the latter. Burke, however, while conceding a distinction *in thought* between the universal and the particular, doesn't seem to think that any such sharp ontological distinction exists *in reality*. Instead, I suggest that for Burke, *in knowing the particular, we know the universal*. In other words, every universal is particularized, and every particular is universalized. There is nothing mysterious about this. Every particular is a particular *this* or a particular *that*. But in order to distinguish *this* from *that*, we must recognize the *kinds* of things with which we're dealing. In doing so, we are recognizing *at once* the particular *and* the universal. The difference between the knowledge of the particular and that of the universal is that the former is conscious and explicit while the latter is less so. Yet it is by way of becoming ever more familiar with the particular—Burke's "first principle (the germ, as it were) of public affections"—that we thrust our knowledge of the universal to conscious awareness.

Second, what we know when we know the universal is not God or a process or a force but moral *truths* that we can and often do speak of in terms of "principles" or "ideals." As to the nature of the universal so understood, I will return momentarily.

Thirdly, we know the universal and the particular through experience, yes, but not that of the individual alone, but the experience of many generations, "the general bank and capital of nations and of ages." In other words, moral knowledge is knowledge gained by way of *tradition*.

The claims of Strauss and his ilk aside, to concede that moral knowledge is relative to one's tradition is not to concede relativ*ism* or nihilism. For that matter, neither is it to concede something called "traditionalism." [188] Immanuel Kant, who sought a synthesis of rationalism and empiricism, famously said that just because knowledge *begins* with experience doesn't mean that it all *arises* from experience.[189] Similarly, on this reading of Burke, we can say that just because moral knowledge begins with tradition doesn't mean that it consists only of one's own tradition.

Burke's conception of the English Constitution indicates his awareness of this fact, of the universal particularized. The "mode of existence" possessed by the English tradition is that of "a permanent body composed of transitory parts," a "whole" that, "is never old or middle-aged or young, but, in a condition of unchangeable constancy" and which "moves on through the varied tenor of perpetual decay, fall, renovation, and progression." Its endurance is due to its "stupendous wisdom," a wisdom that both reflects and drives centuries and millennia worth of "moulding together the great mysterious incorporation of the human race [.]" [190] Notice, the English tradition encapsulates, then, not just the experience of the English, but of "the human race." It is a unity-in-difference, a one composed of many, a whole whose identity derives from, not some immutable core or essence, but the gradual and orderly transitions of its parts.

Like the Rationalist-Universalists against whom he rails, Burke too not infrequently speaks of "principles," including and notably, principles of "natural rights." And like his opponents, Burke envisions these principles as having universal jurisdiction. Yet these principles, if conceived as subsisting independently of and prior to civilization, in "all the nakedness of metaphysical abstraction," [191] not only lack self-evidence; they can hardly be said to be even knowable at all, for they have no bearing upon the daily life of the "civil social man." [192] In stark contrast, the universal *particularized*, concretized in the complex of contingencies of which tradition is composed, is both knowable and indispensable to the moral life. Yet what *is* the ontological standing of principles as Burke conceives them?

Burke gives us a suggestion as to what he has in mind when he writes that he does not deny "the *real* rights of men." [69] [193] The latter are threatened by the "pretended rights" of Rationalist-Universalists, for they are determined not a priori, but by the nature of "civil society" itself. Members of the latter, according to Burke, have a right to live by the law; "justice;" "the fruits of their industry, and to the means of making their industry fruitful;" "the acquisitions of their parents" and "the nourishment and improvement of their offspring;" and "instruction in life and…consolation in death." In society, "whatever each man can separately do, without trespassing upon others, he has a right to for himself; and he has a right to a fair portion of all which society, with all its combinations of skill and force, can do in his favor." [194]

Burke's moral principles here, though universal in scope, are discerned in, or abstracted from, reflection on the particularities of tradition.

The objection that unless we view principles as subsisting independently of and prior to history and culture we will be left with "relativism" or "nihilism" reflects the fundamentally wrong-headed conception of a "principle" that the Rationalist-Universalist assumes. But there are three replies ready at hand.

First, even if he is correct and moral principles are the

ahistorical, timeless verities of the Rationalist-Universalist's imaginings, we would be utterly incapable of either knowing or using them. The "self-evidence" that Rationalist-Universalists typically ascribe to their principles is an invention meant to circumvent this problem. It fails: That I am awake while I type this is self-evident, but that all human beings have "rights" to life, liberty, and so forth, is anything but that. As Alasdair MacIntyre has written, there was no word *in any language* for "a right" until about the year 1400. As MacIntyre says, while this doesn't show that there are no natural rights, it does establish that if there are, no one could've known it.[1957] And it proves that these alleged principles of natural right are most definitely *not* self-evident, at least not to us.

The notion of a moral principle would be as inconceivable to a person who wasn't already a moral being shaped by his familiarity with the concreteness, the countless nuances, of his moral tradition as would the notion of a grammatical principle be inconceivable to a person who wasn't already a linguistic being, shaped by the intricacies of his language.

Second, contrary to conventional wisdom, no one "applies" general or universal abstract moral principles to specific situations. Such principles are not "applicable," for even when we are aware of them, this knowledge alone means little to nothing: a general principle considered in abstraction is inherently incapable of specifying which course of action an agent should take *here* and *now*. Like Burke said, it is "circumstances" that "give in reality to every political principle its distinguishing color and discriminating effect."[196] To suggest that the moral life involves applying moral principles to one particular situation after the other is like saying that every speech-act consists in the application of grammatical principles to one particular utterance after the other. It is knowledge, not of abstract universals, but of the concrete details of one's circumstances—a knowledge that *includes* the knowledge of one's tradition—that informs conduct.

Finally, that there is a plurality of moral traditions no

more precludes commerce between them than a plurality of languages precludes the speakers of different languages from dialoguing with one another. Not only is mutual understanding not imperiled by the fact that moral traditions are diverse; mutual understanding is possible only *because* we belong to various traditions: That I'm able to understand and appreciate the achievements and values of *your tradition* derives from my familiarity with *my own*. In turn, in learning about your tradition, I learn more about mine. In learning from one another, we learn together.

Conclusion

I have argued that while neoconservatives and conservatives both affirm patriotism, doing so is inconsistent with the epistemological and ontological commitments of the former: The Rationalism and Universalism of neoconservatives actually require them to regard patriotism, the love of or devotion to one's country, as a vice. In contrast, upon examining the Burke of the *Reflections,* I show that the philosophical suppositions of the conservatism that he articulates must render patriotism a virtue. Yet I also argue that even though he rejects the Rationalism and Universalism of his opponents, and even though particularity figures centrally in his moral vision, Burke endorses universality as well. Far from precluding a love of humanity, the love of one's country—like devotion to all of one's "little platoons"—fosters it, for epistemologically and metaphysically, the universal and the particular are one, for Burke.

Jack Kerwick

Chapter 4

CONSERVATISM AND RACE: "BLACK HETERODOXY"

Introduction

FOR QUITE SOME time, at least since the 1970's, there has been much chatter about the curious phenomenon designated as "black conservatism," an intellectual orientation held by a minority of black thinkers.[197] In what follows, I argue that while there is indeed a "black conservatism," the orientation so-called is actually quite intellectually diverse, encompassing a multiplicity of passages of thought, conservatism being but one. In addition to classical conservatism, what is popularly known as "black conservatism" is constituted as well by strains of classical liberal or "libertarian" and neoconservative thought.[198] Since that which unites those black figures associated with "black conservatism" is a shared conviction that the prevailing leftist racial orthodoxy—what we can call "black orthodoxy"—suffers from a debilitating intellectual and moral impoverishment, I conclude that "black conservatism" should more aptly be recognized as "black heterodoxy."

This paper is divided into four sections. In the first, I select for attention the work of George S. Schuyler and

Thomas Sowell as illustrative of the "traditional" or "classical" conservatism of black heterodoxy. In the second section I highlight its classical liberal elements by examining some of the writings of Walter E. Williams, followed by the third in which I discuss its neoconservative component by analyzing the thought of Alan Keyes.

Classical Conservatism

For over two centuries, conservatives in the Anglo-American tradition, from Burke to David Hume, James Stephens to Joseph DeMaistre, F.A. Hayek to Michael Oakeshott,[199] have unabashedly opposed the *rationalism*[200] of their competitors. The term "rationalism" has assumed an array of meanings depending on the contexts in which it has been situated, but the rationalism with which conservative thinkers have been at odds is a peculiar conception of knowledge in terms of which human reason is assigned vast powers in scope and magnitude, a reservoir of virtually unlimited potential the realization of which vitally depends upon a willingness to accept only those ideas that can be "justified" before "the bar" that it supplies.

In short, the rationalist believes that knowledge *must* be conscious, the product of a reflective engagement susceptible to explicit excogitation in propositional terms and capable, theoretically at least, of being enlisted in the service of bringing to fruition any number of desirable purposes. From this perspective, reason is at once universal and omnipotent, the standard by which tradition, custom, and habit, the "merely" temporary, local, and transitory are to be judged.

Inseparable from this vision of knowledge is a vision of morality that, in spite of having come under fire from various quarters from the time of its emergence until the present day, continues to exert considerable influence. From this perspective, morality is comprised of *principles* and *ideals* that, by virtue of finding their specification in a universal reason, are themselves *universal*. Among such rationalistic moral doctrines are the doctrines of "individualism," "pluralism," "natural rights," "human rights," "principle of utility," "categorical imperative," and "social contract." Conservatives don't necessarily deny that, for convenience's sake if nothing else, such rationalistic language is not without its uses, and they certainly deny neither the desirability nor even the indispensability of ideals and principles to any adequate morality. It isn't, then, principles and ideals *as such* that conservatives reject but, rather, *the rationalist's view of them*. Principles and ideals, from the conservative perspective, are abstractions constructed from the resources of a tradition of conduct—not timeless features of a trans-cultural, tradition-neutral intellect. They are the products, not the begetters, of tradition.[201]

The French revolutionaries and their *philosophes* advanced "the Rights of Man," the archetypical rationalistic moral ideology. It was against this doctrine that Burke railed and in response to which he formulated what would come to be recognized as "modern conservatism." While he not only didn't deny, but actually affirmed natural rights, Burke essentially insisted that their invocation had no place in political society given that "the objects of society are of the greatest possible complexity," a "gross and complicated mass of human passions and concerns."

The natural rights to which his rivals incessantly appeal Burke derisively refers to as "metaphysic rights" and "pretended rights," "extremes" that, "in proportion as they are metaphysically true," are "morally and politically false."[202]

The only rights allusions to which are appropriate in connection to civil society are culturally constituted. Burke describes them in terms of our "inheritance," an "image of a relation of blood" that has the twofold advantage of bolstering "the fallible and feeble contrivances of our reason" by assimilating "the Constitution of our country with our dearest domestic ties," as well as furnishing "a sure principle of conservation," "a sure principle of transmission," and "a principle of improvement." [203]

David Hume too mocked the notion that there are "moral relations, discovered by reason, in the same manner as we discover by reason the truths of geometry or algebra." [204] Moral knowledge is not derivable from "a chain of argument and induction," "metaphysical reasonings," or "deductions from the most abstract principles of the understanding." On the contrary, that which is "honorable," "fair," "becoming," "noble," and "generous," appeals not to the intellect but, rather, "takes possession of the heart, and animates us to embrace and maintain it." [205] While Burke set his sights on the rationalistic doctrine of "the Rights of Man," Hume relentlessly subjected for interrogation the characteristically rationalist idea that the legitimacy of government must be rooted in consensual foundations. This "social contract" theory Hume derides as a fiction, insisting that it is by way of habit or custom that government achieves its authority. "Obedience or subjection becomes so familiar, that most men never make any enquiry about its origins or cause, more than the principle of gravity, resistance, or the most universal laws of nature." [206]

The rationalist's ideal conception of a reason unencumbered by such parochial constraints as those imposed by the likes of tradition, custom, and habit, in conjunction with the principles/ideals-oriented universalistic vision of morality with which it is indissolubly linked, inform his or her conception of the State.

The State, the rationalist holds, derives its justification from the extent to which it succeeds in realizing some ideal or set of ideals accessible to reason and believed to exist in advance of its activities: Freedom, Equality, Prosperity, Justice, Happiness, and Security are alike ideals toward the implementation of which the rationalist holds it is the duty of the State to deploy its resources. This explains the rationalist's proclivity for utopian schemes.

Conservatism, in glaring contrast, being acutely aware of the limitations of the individual's reason and the communal—

i.e., local—character of morality, is staunchly anti-utopian. Ideals are abbreviations of a tradition of conduct that is itself largely unreflectively engaged in by those whose tradition it is. That it is to a significant extent uncritically partaken of is what in large measure insures its vitality and perpetuation. Yet once the provisional abridgments of a tradition are mistaken for self-subsistent ends to which the tradition itself is subordinate and in the service of which all of society's activities are to be enlisted, then the individuality and plurality that the conservative cherishes and which depend on communal tradition are imperiled. Utopian promises, thus, can't be anything other than illusory, for all such efforts to fulfill them must necessarily culminate in the impairment of precisely that which makes social life possible: tradition.

George S. Schuyler

George Schuyler was quite possibly among the greatest editorialists that America ever produced. Born in 1895 in Rhode Island, Schuyler lived in Syracuse, New York with his family until he was old enough to enlist in the United States Army. Upon the completion of World War I, he returned to civilian life, taking up residence in Harlem, where he remained until his death in 1977. It was during the decade of the 1920's when, from a thirst for intellectual stimulation rather than the appeal of its ideas, Schuyler joined the Socialist Party and began to travel within circles that would subsequently be identified with "the Harlem Renaissance." It was also during this decade that he began establishing for himself a rapidly expanding reputation as a writer.

Throughout his life, in addition to authoring what has been called the first black science fiction novel, *Black No More*, Schuyler wrote as well for a plethora of other publications, black and white, including *American Mercury*, founded and edited by H.L. Mencken, the largest of literary giants of that time. He was a tireless champion for racial equality and a vehement opponent of communism. From 1922 until 1964, he was the editor for *The Pittsburg Courier,* the largest black newspaper publication in the country. In 1966, Schuyler composed his autobiography, *Black and Conservative.*

Although Schuyler never explicitly spoke of "rationalism," and while he, not unlike any of the black dissidents discussed in this paper, was not a professional philosopher, from his writings it is possible to extract some of the very same themes that have pervaded the literature on conservatism from Burke's day onward.

During the decade of the 1920's, when there was much talk of the "Harlem Renaissance," Schuyler mocked the notion of a distinct "Negro art." He wrote: "Negro art there has been, is, and will be among the numerous black nations of Africa; but to suggest the possibility of any such development among the ten million colored people in this republic is self-evident foolishness." [207]

That American blacks have produced "slave songs based on Protestant hymns and Biblical texts known as the spirituals, work songs and secular songs of sorrow and tough luck known as the blues," jazz, and "the Charleston" are undeniable facts; however, these art forms "are contributions of a caste in a certain section of the country" and, as such, "foreign to Northern Negroes, West Indian Negroes, and African Negroes." This means that they are as "expressive or characteristic of the Negro race" as "the music and dancing of the Appalachian highlanders or the Dalmatian peasantry are expressive or characteristic of the Caucasian race."

Schuyler insists that the music of American blacks, as well as the other arts upon which black artists were credited with stamping a unique impress, are, ultimately, Eurocentric. As he put the matter, "the Aframerican is merely a lampblacked Anglo-Saxon." Schuyler writes:

> The dean of the Aframerican literati is W.E.B. Du Bois, a product of Harvard and German

> *universities; the foremost Aframerican sculptor is Meta Warwick Fuller, a graduate of leading American art schools and former student of Rodin; while the most noted Aframerican painter, Henry Ossawa Tanner, is dean of painters in Paris and has been decorated by the French Government.*[208]

Noting that none of this should be of any surprise considering that "the Aframerican is subject to the same economic and social forces that mold the actions and thoughts of the white Americans," Schuyler continues:

> *In the homes of the black and white Americans of the same cultural and economic level one finds similar furniture, literature, and conversation. How, then, can the black American be expected to produce art and literature dissimilar to that of the white American?*[209]

I submit that throughout this essay—one written very early on in his career—Schuyler exhibits an acute, characteristically conservative sensitivity to the indispensable role that culture or tradition plays in shaping and even constituting the individuality, the intellectual horizons, of those who can claim it as their own, a sensitivity that would pervade his thought throughout the remainder of his life.

Radical individualism, the notion that anyone can transcend the habits, dispositions, mores, and traditions of the society from within which he or she was nurtured, is a species of rationalism, and although those on whom Schuyler sets his sights make no such assertions on the part of the individual as such but, rather, the race to which individuals belong, claims on behalf of "self-made" racial groups shedding the cultural contexts within which they developed are no less fantastic and no less rationalistic then tales of "self-made" individuals recreating themselves *de novo*.

Four decades later, Schuyler continued to stress the inexorability of culture in determining the self-understanding, whether severally or collectively, of American blacks. The variety of "Back to Africa" movements that have proliferated since the days of the American Colonization of Society have all failed, Schuyler explains, because, again, "the American Negro" has vastly more in common with his white brethren in the United States than he shares with non-Americans of the same or darker skin pigmentation. Although "their training and education would undoubtedly be helpful to the backward and newly-emergent states" throughout the Third World, "barriers of language and culture" insure that black Americans "in large numbers would not be accepted today anywhere on earth....." [210] As for their acceptance in Africa, Schuyler writes:

> *Soil depletion, desiccation and the general impoverishment and ignorance of quarreling ethnic groups indigenous to the Dark Continent make it most unappealing to people whose standard of living is in general superior to that of Europeans, to say nothing of Africans.*

"American Negroes" have "nothing whatever in common with even the most advanced Africans....." [211]

This keen understanding of and deep appreciation for the tradition-constituted character of knowledge, individuality, and morality finds direct expression in Schuyler's argument against what would come to be known as the Civil Rights Act of 1964. It is his subscription to this classically conservative vision that both informs and reflects as well his attitude toward politics, specifically, the sort of *change* that is both possible and desirable for government to try to affect. His position on change also squarely locates Schuyler clearly within the classical conservative tradition.

Schuyler invokes several considerations against the Civil Rights Bill, but the essence of his position is that it is of a piece "of largely unenforceable legislation" that "has everywhere been characteristic of political immaturity." This "political immaturity" is almost invariably coupled with "a passion for novelty" that inspires in the country that it inflicts a propensity "to speed social change by law," a disposition that in turn is rooted in the assumption that "it is possible to make people better by *force*."

Yet this last supposition and the willingness to act on it have "been the cause of much misery and injustice throughout the ages." A country like America is especially prone to be seized by this "passion for novelty," for it is a "young nation" that "grew out of conquest, immigration, revolution and civil war....."[212] Notice, Schuyler is under no illusion that America is unique among the nations of the world in allegedly having been founded, all at once, as it were, on an "idea," "ideal," or "proposition," for he was well aware of the fact that it owes its origins to the very same sorts of "accidents" of history by which every other country emerged.

If they are to be durable and beneficial, changes in race relations, like all social changes, cannot be abruptly *designed* by legislators availing themselves of the State's apparatus of power but, instead, transpire gradually in accordance with the habits and sensibilities of the majority of its citizens. Change, in other words, must be orderly if the ostensible ends of the legislation proposed are to escape being undermined. Schuyler succinctly states: "It is axiomatic that it takes lots of time to change social mores, especially with regard to such hardy perennials as religion, race and nationality, to say nothing of social classes."[213] Insofar as legislation fails to accommodate the habits and customs of those to whom it pertains, "the more difficult and expensive" will its enforcement be, and "the less popular," the less legitimate, will the government become.

Schuyler spent his life addressing the treatment to which

American blacks had been subjected by their fellow Americans, and even while arguing against passage of the proposed Civil Rights Bill, he makes unmistakable his contempt for the oppression under which blacks had been made to labor. The majority's attitude toward black Americans "is morally wrong, nonsensical, unfair, un-Christian and cruelly unjust...." However, while "changes have been very slow since 1865" when blacks were finally emancipated from slavery, what changes have occurred "have been marked," and "civil rights laws, state or federal, have had little to do with it." These civil rights laws "have been enforced and accepted only when the dominant majority acquiesced, and have generally lain dormant in the law books." That is, "*custom* has dictated the pace of compliance." [214]

Schuyler's "principal case" against this Civil Rights bill is anchored in his affirmation of liberty. But the liberty to which he appeals is not an abstraction, a trans-cultural, trans-historical, timeless Right or Ideal, but the concrete institutional arrangements of American society, specifically its federalist constitutional framework and the wide dispersal of power of which it consists.

"The principal case against a federal Civil Rights law is the dangerous purpose it may serve. It is still another encroachment by the central government on the federalized structure of our society...Under such a law the individual everywhere is told what he must do and what he cannot do, regardless of the laws and ordinances of his state or community. This is a blow at the very basis of American society which is founded on state sovereignty and individual liberty and preference." [215]

That is, it is the liberty implied in our constitution, not the liberty expressly proclaimed in the Declaration of Independence, that Schuyler invokes.

In his autobiography, Schuyler corrects the rationalistic tendency on the part of his opponents to judge America in the light of an ideal of justice; instead, he remarks, all judgments must be in terms, not of unrealized possibilities, but actual realities. The insistence that in politics the focus be on the concrete and actual rather than the abstract and ideal is a hallmark of conservative thought that we might describe as its vehement anti-utopianism. Among the multiracial nations of the Earth, contrary to her critics, America is "dealing better" with its racial challenges than any other. Schuyler asserts that while "it was all well and good to expect more of America than any other country," it must be remembered that what "was an American problem was also a global one from which no country was free." In fact, "it is in a way indicative of the superior position of the Negro in America that he has such rising expectations, elsewhere chiefly non-existent, save among a tiny minority of the better circumstanced." [216]

In summation, Schuyler's thought is representative of classical conservatism, for like his predecessors stretching back to Burke, he argued against the rationalistic doctrines of his liberal, socialist, and communist rivals by invoking tradition and culturally-centered conceptions of knowledge, morality, and politics. The expanse of the individual's intellectual horizons and moral potentialities, Schuyler asserted, like the possibilities that exist for societies, far from being determined by eternal principles or ideals that are alleged to subsist in advance of social practices, are in reality the latter's products. Thus, political or social change, whether it is change in race relations or any other kind, cannot be advantageously achieved unless it is intimated by and, hence, readily incorporated by, tradition.

Thomas Sowell

Thomas Sowell is by trade an economist whose area of specialization is the history of economic thought. Born in Charlotte, North Carolina in June of 1930, he moved to Harlem with extended family members when he was nine. Upon quitting high school, Sowell left home and joined the army where he subsequently acquired an interest in photography. When returning to civilian life, he decided to pursue a higher education, first at Howard University, and then at Harvard, where he graduated with honors. Sowell decided to pursue graduate studies and in the late 1960's he was awarded a doctoral degree in economics from the University of Chicago. Throughout his career, he has authored over 30 books and numerous journal articles, and for over the last 20 years he has been a nationally syndicated columnist. Although he is an economist by profession, Sowell has written extensively with respect to all manner of issues—especially race, an area on which he has brought his knowledge of economics to bear.[217]

Sowell has spent most of his professional life exposing the follies of rationalism, as they pertain both to issues that are racially oriented as well as those that are not obviously so, yet it his seminal *Knowledge and Decisions* that is a tour-de-force against this "treacherous" intellectual disposition.[218] Rationalism "accepts only what can 'justify' itself to 'reason'— with reason being narrowly conceived to mean articulated specifics." But the "highly rational intellectual 'models' of human behavior" that comprise rationalism "suffer from an air of unreality," a fact that is readily witnessed as soon as the "hypothetical, computer-like incremental adjustments by coolly calculating decision makers" on which they rely "are compared to the flesh-and-blood reality of decision by inertia, whim, panic, or rule of thumb."[219]

Rationalism admits of a multiplicity of variations but all versions are guilty of committing what Sowell describes as "the animistic fallacy," the belief that all instances of order are "the result of purposeful activity toward the goal achieved...." The animistic fallacy has an extensive and storied past, having made appearances in a wide variety of human disciplines. This should come as no surprise, for "perhaps the simplest and most psychologically satisfying explanation of any observed phenomenon is that it happened that way because someone wanted it to happen that way." [220] Sowell states that generally speaking, the rationalistic terms in which inter-group disparities are explained lead to the animistic fallacy, for whether they invoke such notions as "ability," "merit," or "discrimination," cultural considerations are equally excluded. "'Ability" or 'discrimination' are thus among the first explanations seized upon" to account for these inequalities, "much as primitive man explained the rustling of leaves by someone's deliberate moving of them."

However, once it is clear that results observable at a given point in time may be part of a process that stretches far back in time, it is no longer automatically necessary that the current situation be a result of either meritorious or unworthy actions by contemporaries—either group members or others.

Sowell concludes:

> *Differences in cultural values, for example, have deep roots in centuries past and profound impact on current behavior.* [221]

Culture, according to Sowell, far from being the product of deliberate design, is "an evolutionary product," by which he means "an ecology of human relations" that has been centuries and even millennia in the making. From this anti-rationalistic perspective—Sowell calls it "evolutionism"—"it is by no means clear that any and all well-articulated reasons for changing particular parts of this social ecology must be valid." The problem is that "articulated rationality can seldom predict very far or very specifically," and so "a policy's unintended consequences throughout a complex system is a weighty consideration." [222] It is of vital importance that our cultural traditions not be undermined, for "culture provides a wide range of beliefs, attitudes, preferences, and customs" [223] on which millions of human beings rely for their activities.

In *The Vision the Anointed,* Sowell elaborates on this understanding of cultural tradition, as well as the conception of change that it entails. While change is an inexorable fact of life, societies should proceed with great caution when attending to it, opting for changes that are small and gradual over those that are large and dramatic, for "barbarism is...an ever-present threat when the civilizing institutions are weakened or undermined." [224] Sowell frequently and approvingly alludes to Burke, whose "sense of the fragility of civilization led" the latter to "regard the promotion of social experimentation and atomistic reason as a dangerous playing with fire." [225] The problem is that the rationalist's epistemological and moral conceptions—"the notion that 'society' must justify itself before the bar of 'reason'"—implies "that there is some individual or group capable of such encyclopedic knowledge" [226] as to supply "solutions" to all of society's problems. This is the rationalist's dream.

Given his anti-utopianism, Sowell unabashedly declares that "there are no 'solutions'....only trade-offs," a fact of the human condition that promises that "many desires" will remain "unfulfilled" and there will continue to be "much unhappiness in the world."

The twofold challenge posed to us is "how to make the best trade-offs from the limited options available," and how to achieve the "realization that 'unmet needs' will necessarily remain," for "attempting to fully meet these needs *seriatim* only deprives other people of other things, so that a society pursuing such a policy is like a dog chasing its tail." Thus, "particular solutions to particular problems are far less important than having and maintaining the right processes for making trade-offs and correcting inevitable mistakes." [227]

Sowell's tradition-based vision of reason, knowledge, morality, and politics establishes, I have argued, that like Schuyler before him, he is a conservative in the tradition of Burke.

Classical Liberalism

The name "classical liberalism" has today been largely replaced by "libertarianism." Doubtless this is in no small part because "liberalism" has come to be associated with a political-moral ideology that, in spirit if not in every detail, bears few if any similarities to that to which the term historically referred. Regardless of this alteration in nomenclature, and irrespective of the reasons that account for it, I will here continue to refer to this political philosophical vision by its original name.

Though in the seventeenth and eighteenth centuries, when it originated, classical liberalism had its share of eloquent exponents, the British philosopher John Locke provided what would become widely recognized as among its most distinguished defenses. If Burke is classical conservatism's "patron saint," then Locke is classical liberalism's.

According to Locke, the State or government must be rooted in contractual foundations. More specifically, only if the government has the *consent* of the governed can it claim legitimacy. Locke invoked a device common to social contract theorists of his time, namely, "the state of nature," a pre-political condition in which individuals have both "perfect freedom to order their actions and dispose of their possessions and persons," as well as "equality, wherein all the power and jurisdiction is reciprocal, no one having more than another." [228]

Because this "state of nature" has its share of limitations, human beings eventually abandon it and, from enlightened self-interest, agree to form political society. But this transition doesn't alter their realization that by nature they are and always will be "free and equal," for it is "reason" that "teaches all mankind, who will but consult it, that being all equal and independent, no one ought to harm another in his life, health, liberty, or possessions," [229] goods to which all human beings have divinely endowed rights that Jefferson would later describe as "unalienable." And since, Locke states, all persons are "by nature all free, equal, and independent, no one can be put out of this estate, and subjected to the political power of another, without his own consent."[230]

The stark differences between the classical conservative vision and Lockean-style classical liberalism must not go unnoticed. The latter's atavistic conceptions of reason and individuality, abstract and timeless understanding of "natural rights," and ahistorical account of the origins and legitimacy of government, reveals it as a variety of precisely that orientation with respect to which classical conservatism has always been the antithesis: rationalism. This point must be made not in order to determine the one perspective intellectually superior to the other, but so that the philosophical diversity among the black heterodox may be brought to light.

Walter E. Williams

Walter E. Williams was born in Philadelphia, Pennsylvania in 1936. While a toddler, his father abandoned his mother, leaving her to raise Walter and his sister in the Richard Allen Homes Housing Project. In the late 1950's, Williams was drafted into military service. Upon being discharged, he pursued collegiate studies, and in the 1970's he earned his doctoral degree in economics from the University of California at Los Angeles. Williams is an economics professor at George Mason University, the author of several books and numerous journal articles, and a nationally syndicated columnist.

In his *Do the Right Thing*, a collection of his columns, Williams unambiguously explains his "values system."

At the root of my values system is the principle of natural law as expounded by philosophers like John Locke and William Blackstone and adopted by early American notables such as Thomas Jefferson, James Madison, George Mason, Patrick Henry, and Thomas Paine, among others, and captured so simply, elegantly, and compellingly in our Declaration of Independence in the phrase:

> *We hold these truths to be self-evident, that all men are created equal, that they are endowed by their Creator with certain unalienable rights, that among these are Life, Liberty and the Pursuit of Happiness.* [231]

Notice, Williams considers himself a proponent of natural law, but this is not the natural law of such pre-modern, classical and medieval thinkers as Augustine and Aquinas, but the peculiarly modernistic construal of natural law characteristic of such rationalistic thinkers as Locke, Jefferson, Patrick Henry, and Thomas Paine. That is, unlike Sowell, for instance, with whose thought his is usually identified, Williams draws philosophical inspiration from a tradition of thinkers whose cast of mind classical conservatives of a Burkean persuasion have always fiercely resisted.

Locke's impress upon Williams' exposition of natural law is unmistakable. "The first principle of natural law," he states, "holds that each person owns himself." Self-ownership follows from the fact that "in the state of nature, without government, all people are free and equal *but* insecure." The insecurity that is our condition in the state of nature owes to the fact "that other people may not respect our self-ownership rights and, through intimidation, threats, and coercion, wrongly confiscate our property and violate our persons." Due to this precarious situation, people leave the state of nature and "form governments granting them certain limited powers."

Since, though, by nature we are (equally) free and equal, "we all have the right to protect ourselves, family, and property from encroachment by others." So, "when our rights to life, liberty, and property are violated, we have the right to be prosecutor, judge, jury, and, if need be, executioner." Thus, to the governments that we form "we grant these rights…in exchange for the guarantee that the state will perform these security functions." In other words: "We give up only the rights necessary for government to perform its only function—protecting our security." [232]

Williams charges fellow Americans with abandoning "those basic ideals and principles on which our prosperous nation was built"—ideals, for example, like Freedom—for the sake of "other ideals, such as equality of income, sex and race balance, orderly markets, consumer protection, energy conservation, and environmentalism, just to name a few...." [233] However, in order to achieve these latter goals government must "confiscate...through intimidation, threats, and coercion," the resources of some citizens so as to redistribute them to others. Yet if such methods "are clearly an affront to human rights when done privately," then they are no less a violation of human rights when appropriated by a collectivity—even if that collectivity is the government acting by "legal sanctions" or on behalf of "the majority." [234]

Americans must ask whether an act clearly immoral and criminal when done privately becomes moral when done collectively and given legal sanction. The unambiguous answer will be that legality is a poor guide to morality. After all, slavery and apartheid were legal, as were the Nazi persecution of Jews and the Stalinist and Maoist purges. But the fact of being legal did not make them moral acts.[235]

"Immoral laws," Williams bluntly asserts, "aren't worthy of obedience." [236]

Among those immoral laws that Williams believes demand disobedience are those criminalizing "vices." He writes: "For the government to declare a vice a crime is to violate those natural law guarantees of life, liberty, and pursuit of happiness, which are enunciated in our Declaration of Independence." [237] Since no individual has "the right" to punish others for their vices, government must lack this right, for whatever rights government possesses it derives from its citizens.

Williams laments that "these principles of natural law that played such an important role in the framers' thinking about our Constitution are held in high contempt by Congress, the courts, and...most Americans." He is especially troubled by the fact "that black Americans share so much of this generalized contempt and eagerly advocate and participate in the attack against the principles of natural law," for "blacks, more than any other Americans, should love and respect natural law and have the deepest suspicions of government," particularly a government that was guilty of perpetrating "the abuses of Reconstruction and Jim Crow" that "were rooted in disrespect for natural law."[238]

Williams, I have shown, is *not* a conservative, but a classical liberal of a Lockean sort. He articulates his political-moral vision in the same rationalistic idiom within which his welfare-state liberal and socialist opponents frame theirs. Both Williams and his adversaries construe morality primarily in terms of "principles" and "ideals," ostensibly trans-cultural goals upon which human societies are "founded" and in the service of which they must be enlisted. Williams invokes "natural law," a purportedly universal code of morality comprised of self-evident and abstract propositions—"Rights"; "the state of nature," a condition of relatively peaceful co-existence between individual persons prior to the formation of political or civil society; and a contractually-based notion of the State according to which only those governments that have elicited the consent of its citizens and safeguard their "inalienable rights to life, liberty, property, and the pursuit of happiness" are legitimate and, thus, deserving of obedience.

Neoconservatism

There is a third type of black heterodoxy that is neither classically conservative nor classically liberal. For lack of a better term, I will call it neoconservatism. Since relative to the classical conservative and liberal traditions neoconservatism is a relatively new political philosophical orientation, the scholarly literature concerning it is comparatively scarce.[239] Another challenge to defining it is that neoconservatism is typically identified as a popular political *movement*, not a philosophical or intellectual tradition. It is usually recognizable in terms of the substance or content of the positions to which its adherents subscribe on contemporary issues of policy. Still, from those positions it is far from impossible to abstract certain mutually (even if not systematically) related formal considerations upon which they are rooted, considerations largely shared by the classical liberalism of which Williams is an exponent and which, thus, expose neoconservatism as another species of rationalism.

Leo Strauss is typically recognized as the chief, or at least original, inspiration of what has subsequently been called neoconservatism. Strauss defends against its "historicist" objectors—by which he means Burke and the conservative thinkers who followed in his wake—a conception of "natural right" that he claims has roots stretching back to the classical era. He writes that "the need for natural right is as evident today as it has been for centuries and even millennia," for "to reject natural right is tantamount to saying that all right is positive, and this means that what is right is determined exclusively by the legislators and the courts of the various countries." [240] According to Strauss, Burke and "the historical school" that the former credits the latter with pioneering were aware of the "necessarily...revolutionary, disturbing, unsettling effect" of the widely held belief in natural rights. Things couldn't be otherwise, for "the recognition of universal principles forces man to judge the established order, or what is actual here and now, in the light of the natural or rational order," an order of which "what is actual here and now is more likely than not to fall short...." [241]

Strauss writes:

> *The recognition of universal principles thus tends to prevent men from wholeheartedly identifying themselves with, or accepting, the social order that fate has allotted to them. It*

> tends to alienate them from their place on the earth. It tends to make them strangers, and even strangers on the earth.²⁴²

For neoconservatives, only "liberal democracies" can insure the protection of "human rights," and the United States is *the* liberal democracy *par excellence*. For this reason, Francis Fukuyama asserts that "the United States needs to remain engaged in international affairs," for "American power has been and could be used for moral purposes...." ²⁴³ Allan Bloom, usually credited with being among neoconservatism's principal architects, writes that since "modern philosophy" has established that "political equality" is "the only just system of society," it follows that "there is no intellectual ground remaining for any regime other than democracy." ²⁴⁴ That the United States has a special duty to promote "liberal democracy" should be of no offense to any rational being, least of all those who had no objections to America' involvement in the second World War, for World War II, Bloom believes, "was really an educational project undertaken to force those who did not accept" American "principles of freedom and equality and the rights based on them" to do so. There can be no legitimate reason for not accepting these principles, for they "are rational and everywhere applicable." ²⁴⁵

On its face, neoconservatism appears not all that different from classical liberalism: both presuppose an abstract, universalistic conception of human reason; a trans-cultural, tradition-neutral, principles and/or ideals-based vision of morality; and a global, ideals-driven conception of politics.

Yet there are indeed differences between the two, in terms of both the principles and themes emphasized as well as the conclusions regarding policy issues drawn from those principles. Classical liberals like Williams, as we have seen, argue from principles of natural right to an unambiguously decentralized system of American government that exists to insure a maximal degree of liberty for *its citizens*.

Neoconservatives, while claiming to favor this same kind of liberty, reason that these principles, being timeless and universal, deserve protection by the government not just at home but abroad. This, at any rate, is one key difference between these two perspectives.

Alan Keyes

Admittedly, Keyes doesn't squarely fit into the neoconservative mold. He staunchly rejects the materialistic, secular, socialistic impulses of the dominant ideology of welfare-state liberalism, and unlike classical conservatives, he seems to hold that the State is entrusted with the responsibility of promoting *moral truth*, as opposed to peaceful co-existence between citizens holding a diversity of disparate conceptions of moral truth. Furthermore, Keyes is no classical liberal, for while he affirms the same "inalienable rights" to life, liberty, property, and the pursuit of happiness as the typical classical liberal, he is significantly more likely than the latter to favor substantial governmental intervention, both domestically and internationally, to promote those rights.

Due to these considerations, I contend that it is not with injustice that we associate Keyes with neoconservatism.

The one issue to which Keyes repeatedly speaks is the issue of abortion, of which he is an unequivocal opponent. The immorality of abortion is a recurring theme throughout his essays, and while it seems to occupy a disproportionate amount of space, Keyes explains that his focus on abortion owes not *just* to the gravity of the issue in itself, but "the corruption of our idea of freedom" of which it is emblematic, "a corruption that is really killing us."

If we harden our hearts against our offspring, and if we aggrandize our self-fulfillment to the extent that we are even willing to kill our offspring, that is the extreme case of the self-centered and egotistical and self-worshipping concept of freedom I think is being promoted in various ways in the society.

Abortion is illustrative of that debased notion of freedom according to which there is "the right to destroy the rights of others." [246] Thus, for Keyes, there are but two options of which we can avail ourselves. "We are going to have to decide whether we shall quote the words of the *Declaration of Independence* with real conviction" and "stand by the great principle that declares that all human beings are 'created equal' and 'endowed by their Creator' with 'the right to life,'" or "whether we shall take that document and throw it on the ash heap of history...." [247]

Freedom entails "moral requirements" that are specified in the *Declaration of Independence*, a document that affirms unambiguously that "our freedom comes from a transcendent authority—from the Creator." [248]

Keyes asserts that "the real crisis of our times is...a crisis of character," a crisis engendered "by our inability to admit the moral requirement of freedom," "our insistence on marginalizing Truth." [249] But if we are determined to reject "the idea that there is a foundation in our lives for human justice and the observance of human justice," a Supreme "Source of unalienable rights and the Policeman stationed in every human heart" on the basis of which "the great American experiment in liberty" and the "relatively universal" "moral regime" that it "involved" developed, then it will be at nothing less than the cost of that experiment, the loss of America as we have always known it. [250]

Keyes underscores the Declaration of Independence's affirmation of their divine ground, it is true, but the moral vernacular of rationally self-evident "principles" and "unalienable human rights" in which he speaks reveals his distance from the conservatism with which Keyes is popularly associated. The classical conservative tradition, as we have seen, is decidedly anti-rationalistic, yet the political philosophical orientation to which Keyes subscribes, what I have here identified as neoconservatism, is an expression of rationalism.

While an ambassador to the United Nations, Keyes explains that he often had to engage in the "not too terribly easy" enterprise of defending his position in favor of strong American-Israeli relations, a task the challenges of which arose from the transitory character of the "practical, pragmatic," and "entirely material" considerations in terms of which such defenses were not infrequently made by others. After all, since "the world has an unwieldy way of changing," it is conceivable that "there might even be compelling geo-strategic reasons why we should actually abandon" the U.S.-Israeli alliance.

Yet at "the level of our moral identity," Keyes continues, there is no difficulty at all in justifying America's particularly close relationship with Israel. And what is true of America's connection with Israel can equally be said on behalf of all of the close relationships that she has fostered throughout her history. "When we really get down to it…and we come face to face with the ultimate issues of war and peace," regardless of the countries under discussion, "all of those geo-strategic things go by the boards," a fact amply supported by just a cursory reading of previous presidents' speeches. Such speeches invariably contain "arguments that stir the moral sentiments of this nation, and that call upon our willingness to moral commitments, to the things that we believe are right."[251]

Keyes adds a cautionary note, reminding us that appeals to "moral identity" in supporting America's involvement with other countries presupposes that there is "an understanding of our common moral ground." What is this "common moral ground?"

We must be clear on this: the moral principles that this nation stands on, are not principles lost in the mists of time. They're not things we are making up as we go along. In fact, we know what they are. They were clearly articulated when the nation was founded. They have been at various reprises in our history hallowed with the blood of our patriots, and called upon by those who were living without justice. And they have been used successfully to motivate our will in war and to move our conscience in times of peace, to shape this nation's institutions in light of its better principles.[252]

The "moral principles" on which "this nation stands" are the "self-evident" "truths" that "our Founders set down" and that "still ring down, through our history, with a grand decisiveness," namely, the principle(s) that "all men are created equal" and "endowed by their Creator with certain unalienable rights."

It is these principles that, "in spite of all our human frailty and weakness" and "the whole weight of human history which was against the quest for real justice," nevertheless "we have managed decade by decade through these two centuries and more of our existence to move in the direction of greater and greater respect for justice, liberty, and right." It is these principles that comprise "everything we are," for "everything we claim to be as a free people is summarized in" them.[253] Our "guiding principles" are "our essential selves," so if we "disregard" them "at home," they will "lose credibility and we would lose our will in the struggle to defend them around the world."[254] It is these principles embodied in the Declaration that "give content to our valiant fight for the rest of humankind...."[255]

Keyes exemplifies neoconservative thought. Not unlike his non-black counterparts, he embraces an unencumbered account of reason and a vision of morality no less universalistic and abstract, an ideology of "principles," specifically, inalienable human rights, that it is the responsibility of the American government to ambitiously promote not only at home but globally.

Conclusion

My objective in this essay was to show that the conventional wisdom notwithstanding, "black conservatism" is a misnomer when it is used to identify the political philosophical orientation of a relatively small, but significant, minority of black thinkers who resolutely reject the left-leaning, political orthodoxy of the majority of their brethren, for beyond a contemptuous attitude toward that orthodoxy, they share little else.

Hence, I submit that "black heterodoxy" would be a more appropriate nomenclature. Also, I identified at least three currents of thought within black heterodoxy, classical conservatism, classical liberalism, and neoconservatism, and selected representative thinkers of each. George Schuyler and Thomas Sowell I linked with classical conservatism, Walter Williams with classical liberalism, and Alan Keyes with neoconservatism.

Chapter 5

CONSERVATISM and RACE: THE PHILOSOPHY OF "BLACK CONSERVATIVE" THOMAS SOWELL

Introduction

THERE HAS BEEN much talk in recent of decades of "black conservatism." The term itself is fairly controversial. There are reasons for this, but a thorough investigation of them lies beyond the scope of this paper.[256] Nevertheless, any potentially fruitful discussion of "black conservatism" must be preceded by the following qualifications.

If by "black conservatism" we mean a political orientation of a certain kind that is distinct from all other forms of political conservatism, then there is no such thing as "black conservatism." That there may be blacks who are conservative and who bring the wealth of resources afforded by their intellectual tradition to bear upon their examinations of racial issues no more suffices to establish the existence of a "black conservatism" in the sense just described than the fact that there are blacks who analyze race relations through the conceptual lenses of liberalism establishes the reality of "black liberalism." It is just as true of conservatives as it is of liberals that they can and do come in all colors. Furthermore, just as liberals, irrespective of racial background, have addressed racial issues, so conservatives, black and white (and other), have as well.

There is one more point. Black thinkers invariably described as "black conservatives," [257] though they reject the contemporary liberal dogma on race, are not necessarily "conservative" in the classical sense of that term. That neither their defenders nor their opponents have taken the time to delineate the at times significant philosophical differences between them is unfortunate, for these black critics of the political Left compose anything but a monolith, and even when their views on race converge, they are often informed and motivated by beliefs that are not only logically distinct, but, not infrequently, mutually incompatible.[258]

With all of this in mind, I will argue in what follows that there is indeed at least one genuinely conservative, contemporary American black thinker. That thinker is Thomas Sowell. In this paper, in approaching conservatism as essentially a theory of knowledge through which a peculiar conception of politics is nurtured, I intend to show both that Sowell endorses these conceptions of knowledge and politics and that he brings them to bear upon his examination of racial issues.

This paper is divided into two sections. In the first, I contextualize Sowell's thought by situating it within the conservative intellectual tradition to which it belongs. In the second, I show how Sowell's conservative orientation informs his views on racial issues.

II

Thomas Sowell was born in Charlotte, North Carolina in 1930. At the age of nine, he and his family moved northward to Harlem, where Sowell came of age. He eventually dropped out of high school and joined the United States Marine Corps. When his service with the military ended, Sowell entered

Howard University. Not long afterward, he transferred to Harvard, where he majored in economics. Upon graduation, Sowell embarked upon graduate school, and some years later, he completed the doctoral program in economics at the University of Chicago. In the intervening years, Sowell has taught at several prestigious institutions, including Cornell, Columbia, and Stanford, while cementing his reputation as a preeminent scholar of the history of economic thought. He has long since abandoned teaching, having become, in the 1960's, thoroughly disenchanted with what he perceived to be an increasingly politicized academy. In addition to having worked for a time in the public sector, Sowell has spent the last couple of decades at the Hoover Institution, where he has brought his training in economics to bear upon issues, like race-relations, that haven't traditionally been treated in accordance with conventional economic concepts. At one time a Marxist, Sowell had a political conversion during the sixties when he began to realize that the idealistic assumptions of his youth could not withstand scrutiny. He gradually gravitated away from the political left and toward conservatism.[259]

Before proceeding, it would be appropriate and instructive to momentarily consider what Sowell himself had written on his relationship to conservatism. In so doing, we can both resolve what appears to be a contradiction between his understanding of this matter and the thesis of this essay, as well as illuminate the character of the conservative tradition with which I associate him.

Sowell writes that "if there is one word" that he "would like to see disappear from the English language, that word is 'conservative.'" Why? "It doesn't really mean anything," for it is applied to people like F.A. Hayek, Milton Friedman, Ronald Reagan, and Sowell himself, people "who want to make large and fundamental changes in the way the whole economy and society function."[260] Among the "radical changes" that Sowell would like to implement are the abolition of the office of the Vice President, the elimination of life tenure for federal justices, and a Constitutional amendment that prohibits anyone with income or wealth above the national average from being recipients of government transfer payments. It is because neither he nor any of the other aforementioned individuals are supportive of the political left, Sowell believes, that they are automatically regarded as "conservative." "Everybody who opposes the left agenda," even though "they have nothing in common" with each other—"monarchists and democrats, libertarians and fascists"—is called "'the right'..." Sowell says of this political or ideological situation that it is "Ptolemaic," with "the left in the center and everyone else defined by how they relate to the left." So, if Sowell expressly disavows the term "conservative" as a self-description, on what grounds can I apply it to him?

The contradiction in question is only apparent, and it dissolves as soon as it is realized that Sowell is construing "conservatism" in thoroughly substantive terms. If there was any doubt about this before, he dispels it once and for all in the final sentence of this column. "The time is long overdue to start thinking about specific policies, instead of about labels and rhetoric." [261] Conservatism, though, is first and foremost a primarily *formal* orientation. It is true that with respect to the formal presuppositions that they share, conservatives are likely (yet certainly not guaranteed) to endorse similar policy or substantive prescriptions; but the conservatism with which I am concerned and with which I associate Sowell is largely a formal disposition.[262]

Sowell's point is well taken if he means to suggest that any anthology that addresses conservative thought in its disparate cultural and historical manifestations is bound to contain thinkers who share little if anything in the way of substance with one another,[263] but this is *no* support for his contention that "conservatism" is a meaningless word. By this standard, "the left," "liberalism," "Aristotelianism," "Thomism," and any number of words on which we rely to distinguish one school of thought from all others are equally meaningless, for each of the groups that they designate admit of substantive variations comparable in quantity and quality to conservatism. As I will show, when conservatism is understood as theorists of conservatism have understood it—as a basically formal orientation—Sowell is unequivocally a conservative.

Familiarity with the literature on conservatism reveals it to be, in the final resort, a theory of knowledge, more specifically, one that is tradition-centered. There are inescapable limitations on what any individual person can know, much less consciously know. Much, and perhaps most, knowledge is inarticulate, encapsulated in social traditions that have endured centuries, in some cases. All human conduct is made possible by the tradition within which it originates and unfolds. One's worldview arises from the tradition or traditions to which one belongs. From this standpoint, the reason of any individual is constituted and, thus, limited by, the complex tradition to which that individual belongs. What this means is that there is no such thing as Reason as such, an unencumbered, naked, and virtually unlimited power of rationality at least potentially accessible to all people in all places and times, but always a rationality embedded in a culturally-specific nexus of practices. As Edmund Burke famously said:

> *We are afraid to put men to live and trade each on his own private stock of reason; because we suspect that this stock in each man is small, and that the individuals would be better to avail themselves of the general bank and capital of nations, and of ages.*[264]

Twentieth century economist and social theorist F.A. Hayek makes the same point. Hayek cautions us against committing "the fatal conceit," which is "the idea that the ability to acquire skills stems from reason." Rather, he informs us, "it is the other way around: our reason is as much the result of an evolutionary selection process as is our morality." It is our moral traditions that "make possible the growth of reason and those capabilities associated with it." [265] But such traditions "are not justifiable in terms of the canons of traditional theories of rationality." [266] In other words, our moral traditions can never admit of explicit justification, for "the process of selection that shaped customs and morality could take account of more factual circumstances than individuals could perceive…" It is for this reason that Hayek concludes, and here he is at one with Burke who two centuries earlier affirmed "wisdom without reflection and above it," that "tradition is in some respects superior to, or 'wiser' than, human reason." [267]

In his famous essay, "Rationalism in Politics," Michael Oakeshott elucidates further this conception of reason or knowledge. He calls it "practical knowledge," but by this he means knowledge rooted in tradition. Practical knowledge "exists only in use, is not reflective and…cannot be formulated in rules." [268] Oakeshott tells us that since practical knowledge's "normal expression is in a customary or traditional way of doing things, or, simply, in practice," it "can neither be taught nor learned, but only imparted and acquired." [269] Neither Oakeshott nor any other conservative denies the reality of "propositional knowledge." Rather, conservatives insist that propositional knowledge is supplemented by and, more importantly, parasitic upon another type of knowledge, what Oakeshott calls "practical" or "traditional" knowledge. For all intents and purposes, conservative theorists stand alone in affirming knowledge that defies express articulation.

Sowell embraces the conservative vision of the human condition, calling it, alternatively, "constrained" [270] and "tragic." [271] He joins Burke, Oakeshott, Hayek, and any number of other conservative theorists in rejecting without equivocation the atavistic conception of knowledge typical of rationalists. According to the constrained vision, Sowell informs us, any individual's own knowledge alone is grossly inadequate for social decision-making, and often even for his own personal decisions. A complex society and its progress are therefore possible only because of numerous social arrangements which transmit and co-ordinate knowledge from a tremendous range of contemporaries, as well as from the even more vast numbers of those from generations past.

On this account, knowledge is "predominantly *experience*." [272]

The experience to which he alludes is *not* the experience of any individual, but "the social experience of the many, as embodied in behavior, sentiments, and habits," [273] the "traditions which evolve from the day-to-day experiences of millions in each generation..." [274] Sowell often refers to these traditions as "cultural" or "systemic processes," and he speaks to the perennial conservative theme of "second nature" when he says that knowledge—the "multiplicity of experience too complex for explicit articulation" [275]—is "distilled over the generations in cultural processes and traits so deeply embedded as to be virtually unconscious reflexes..." [276] This, he asserts, is what Burke meant when he referred to "wisdom without reflection."

Conservatism's "constrained" conception of individual knowledge—its insistence that the conscious knowledge of any given individual or group of individuals is miniscule relative to the "bank and capital of nations and ages," as Burke put it—accounts for its sympathy with a particular model of the state and society. On this model, society is conceived along the lines of what Oakeshott calls a "civil association" and Hayek describes as a "spontaneously evolved order," by which he means a "free society." Because the knowledge of each individual is severely constrained and presupposes an intricate and open textured tradition of activity the many complex nuances of which, having been unconsciously imbibed, defy explicit articulation, conservatives staunchly oppose the rationalistic notion that society can be compelled to comport with something on the order of a blueprint of supra-temporal ideals. It is this skepticism, in other words, that the conservative holds with respect to both the rationalist's belief in a tradition-neutral, virtually omni-competent Reason, and the perfectionist aspirations that it inspires, that lead the conservative to value individuality and plurality, the two chief characteristics of civil association.

Oakeshott's exposition of "civil association" is as follows. A civil association, he explains, is association with respect to "laws," or "non-instrumental rules of conduct." Laws are "non-instrumental" because "they are not rules that specify a practice or routine purporting to promote the achievement of a substantive purpose," for the members of civil association "have no common substantive purpose." Laws are similar to (though not exactly like) "the rules of a game which are directions, not about how to win but about how to play, or the rules of public debate, which do not tell a speaker what to say and are wholly indifferent to any particular conclusion." He continues: "These non-instrumental rules specify and prescribe, not choices to be made or actions to be performed, but conditions to be subscribed to in choosing and acting."[277]

The rules of civil association can never be considered with respect to their tendency "to promote or hinder the achievement of a common substantive purpose," for in a state conceived as a civil association, "there is none."[278] In a civil association, citizens are regarded as *individuals* who, either severally or in concert with others, are engaged in numerous self-chosen activities. Individuality and plurality are the chief characteristics of a society conceived as a genuinely civil association.[279]

Oakeshott contrasts this conception of society with its rationalist rival: enterprise association. On the model of an enterprise association, the state exists for the sake of bringing to fruition some goal or ideal at least implicitly held to subsist independently of and in advance of the state and in accordance with which its activities are to be evaluated. The terms of an enterprise association can never be anything other than policy prescriptions, orders or commands that derive their significance and justification from their conduciveness in promoting the *telos* that is sought. In the state conceived as an "enterprise association," all members are comrades or partners who must divest at least some of their resources in time, money, and energy to realize the end or plan that is their "common good."

Sowell advocates what Oakeshott calls "civil association," although this is not the idiom that he employs. He contrasts what he calls "traditional justice," on the one hand, with what he describes as "social justice" and "cosmic justice," on the other. We will examine his account of the latter below, but first we must turn to his account of the former. Traditional justice requires that "rules and standards" be "equally applicable to all…" (9).[280] From this standpoint, "justice or injustice is characteristic of a *process*".[281] Sowell submits the example of a criminal trial as an illustration of traditional justice.

A defendant in a criminal case would be said to have received justice if the trial were conducted as it should be, under fair rules and with the judge and jury being impartial. After such a trial, it could be said that "justice was done"—regardless of whether the outcome was an acquittal or an execution. Conversely, if the trial were conducted in violation of the rules and with a judge or jury showing prejudice against the defendant, this would be considered an unfair or unjust trial—even if the prosecutor failed in the end to get enough jurors to vote to convict an innocent person.

Sowell concludes:

> *In short, traditional justice is about impartial processes rather than either results or prospects.*[282]

Although he speaks of justice as a "process," Sowell is of like mind with Oakeshott who denied that in a civil association—a non-purposeful social order—there was any place for substantive considerations of political justice. The "rules and standards equally applicable to all" with respect to which Sowell understands genuine political justice, Oakeshott would say do nothing more (or less) than specify "adverbial conditions" to be observed as citizens engage in their own self-chosen pursuits. As long as government does everything reasonably possible to insure that these conditions are met, justice is done.

Sowell argues against the rationalist project of deliberately enlisting all of society's members in the service of a putative transcendent ideal (Oakeshott's "enterprise association") like Justice—what he calls "cosmic justice." He targets specifically those rationalists who believe that Justice requires the imposition of a substantive condition of material equality, or at least the amelioration, if not the complete elimination, of "'undeserved inequalities.'" The proponents of this view, most of whom have long since abandoned the notion that God is responsible for the numerous statistical disparities of which society is ridden, "are often driven to personify 'society' in order to re-introduce concepts of moral responsibility and justice into the cosmos, seeking to rectify the tragic misfortunes of individuals and groups through collective action..." [283] Ideas of "social justice" or "cosmic justice" that figure prominently among rationalists of all sorts neither Sowell nor the conservative tradition from which he speaks finds intelligible. "Yet," he continues, the "collective action" to which rationalists of this sort are committed "is not limited to correcting the consequences of *social* decisions or other collective social action, but extends to mitigating as well the misfortunes of," for instance, "the physically and mentally disabled...." Such misfortunes are viewed as not arising from society exactly, but "from the cosmos." "It seeks to produce *cosmic* justice...." [284] The main problem with this position, Sowell remarks, is that "the knowledge required to sort...out intellectually, much less rectify...politically" these inequities "is staggering and superhuman." [285] In other words, the goal of cosmic justice is unattainable.

Sowell holds with other conservatives that individuality and plurality are imperiled by the quest for "social" and "cosmic justice," attempts to make society into an enterprise association. He criticizes this "moralism," "the general implicit assumption of a single scale of values applicable to all." [286] Sowell cites the work of John Rawls as illustrative of this line of thought. Rawls insists that as a matter of justice, social and economic goods be "arranged" to the benefit of "the least advantaged." Sowell points out that "the bland and innocuous word 'arrange'" covers "a pervasive exercise of power necessary to supersede innumerable individual decisions," a power wielded in order "to make people stop doing what they want to do and do instead what some given principle imposes." [287] When social justice—a specific value or set of values—is imposed upon the citizenry, "freedom as the general preservation of options gives way to the imposition of one group's preferred option." [288] In other words, "'more' justice in such a world means more forcible imposition of one particular brand of justice—i.e., less freedom." [289]

According to Sowell, rationalists' desire for imposing upon the state the character of an enterprise association arises from the false assumption that it is possible to deliberately *design* a social order that is remotely as efficient in its functioning and, ultimately, beneficial for society as the order that has emerged as the result of millions upon millions of human beings, past and present, habitually, unselfconsciously, following tradition.

The conservative vision that Sowell endorses, however, puts little faith in deliberately designed social processes, since it has little faith that any manageable set of decision-makers could effectively cope with the enormous complexities of designing a whole blueprint for an economic system, a legal system, or a system of morality or politics.

Rather, it "relies instead on historically evolved social

processes and evaluates them in terms of their systemic characteristics—their incentives and modes of interaction—rather than their goals or intentions." [290] Conservatives, in fact, don't think that it is at all meaningful to speak of the "goals or intentions" of "historically evolved social processes" at all. Sowell cites language as the "purest example" of such a process, and just as no one would contend that language has an end or purpose, at least not one specifiable in advance, so no one should think any differently with respect to any other "spontaneously evolved order," to use Hayek's words.

In *The Vision of the Anointed,* Sowell says of language that it "arises out of gropings, accidents, experiences, and historical borrowings and corruptions of other languages," and that its "richness, complexity, and subtleties...have arisen systemically, from the experiences and interactions of millions of ordinary human beings, *not from a top-down 'plan' formulated by some elite.*" Of course, grammarians and linguists are able to reflect upon language in its current condition and codify some of its aspects, but the principles and structures that their investigations reveal are not given in advance of the language but are, rather, its offspring. Specialists can never give us anything more than an abridgement of the language that they seek to explain. "From time to time, linguistic practices are codified or modified by intellectuals, but this is an incidental part of a vast drama." [291] Similarly, political theorists, whether they recognize it or not, do not discover eternal principles or ideals that range over all cultural traditions; rather, the principles or ideals upon which they exposit are abbreviations of their tradition.

It is precisely because of conservatives' painful awareness of the severe limitations on individual human knowledge that they are invariably and exceptionally cautious about pursuing change. It isn't that conservatives are "opposed to" change. It was "the patron saint" of conservatism, Burke, who said that "A state without the means of some change is without the means of its conservation." Rather, conservatives recognize that every change necessarily involves loss, or a "trade-off," as Sowell puts it.

Oakeshott writes that for the conservative, "change…appears always, in the first place, as deprivation." [292] It is not without reservation that he will seek to innovate, for "innovating is an activity which generates not only the 'improvement' sought, but a new and complex situation of which this is only one of the components." In short, "there is no such thing as an unqualified improvement." [293] It is for these reasons that conservatives prefer those innovations that most "resemble growth" over those that strike as being "imposed upon the situation," and changes that are slow and gradual rather than those that are rapid and abrupt.

Sowell endorses this conservative disposition toward change. He notes two possible conceptions of change that he associates with two mutually incompatible "visions." The conservative vision with which he sympathizes he refers to as the "constrained" or "tragic" vision. From this perspective, every change is a "trade-off." In contrast, there is what Sowell calls the "unconstrained vision" or "the vision of the anointed," the vision of rationalists. In *The Vision of the Anointed*, Sowell is to the point: "There are no solutions; there are only trade-offs." [294] All that we have to work with are "trade-offs that still leave many desires unfulfilled and much unhappiness in the world." Thus, "what is needed…is a prudent sense of how to make the best trade-offs from the limited options available," as well as "a realization that 'unmet needs' will necessarily remain…" Sowell cautions against "attempting to fully meet these needs *seriatim*," for it "only deprives other people of other things, so that a society pursuing such a policy is like a dog chasing its tail." He asserts that "particular solutions to particular problems are far less important than having and maintaining the right processes for making trade-offs and correcting inevitable mistakes." [295]

Conservatism is basically a tradition-centered theory of knowledge. The knowledge of any individual is an inheritance from numerous generations of people from throughout the ages, distilled in the tradition(s) to which that individual belongs. Much of this knowledge is unreflective, and even unconscious, and defies explicit excogitation. Because of the severe limitations on individual rationality, because knowledge is largely a matter of (unreflective) practice, conservatives are extremely skeptical of all rationalist plans to usurp "traditional justice" with "social" or "cosmic justice," to replace "plurality" with "homogeneity" by imposing upon society the character of an "enterprise association," rather than a "civil association," a "designed," as opposed to a "spontaneously evolved order." All such rationalistic attempts to "perfect" circumstances presuppose a faith in the possibility of "solutions" that conservatives find incorrigibly naïve. The intractable, unrelenting fallibility of human knowledge guarantees that genuine *solutions* to social problems will forever be beyond our grasp.

I have argued here that despite Sowell's protestation to the contrary, when conservatism is understood properly, as a fundamentally formal disposition, he is indeed located squarely within this tradition. Now I will show how his conservative suppositions are brought to bear upon his analyses of racial issues.

III

The tradition-based (or culture-based) model of politics that conservatives advance differs fundamentally from those models endorsed by rationalists of different stripes. In "Rationalism in Politics," in a footnote, Oakeshott refers to "the politics of Nature" and "the politics of Reason," two equally rationalistic doctrines that, while distinct, overlap in "exceedingly complicated" ways. He says that fundamentally, they share in common a rejection of "civilization," or "all human achievement more than about a generation old." [296] Put another way, regardless of the specific claims made on behalf of each model, or of any of the internal varieties of which they both admit, neither the politics of Nature nor the politics of Reason allots any space to "tradition" ("culture" or "civilization"). This needs to be borne in mind when analyzing Sowell's philosophy of race.

Individuals are not equal; neither are races. The equality to which I refer is not the equality of which Christians have spoken when they have declared, paraphrasing Saint Paul, that all are equal before God. The "moral" or "spiritual" equality of human beings is not in question here. Culturally speaking, neither individuals nor the racial and ethnic groups to which they belong are equal. Proponents of what Sowell calls "the civil rights vision" attribute statistical disparities to "discrimination," or "racism." That is, they assume that such social regularities are deliberately designed by "society." In contrast, others account for these statistical disparities in terms of the genetic advantages and disadvantages of the favored and disfavored groups, respectively. Both positions are expressions of the two forms of rationalism just mentioned, for whether disparities are alleged to be the product of nature or the devious rational design of racists, neither gives the slightest consideration to the role that tradition plays in accounting for these phenomena. Conventional racial orthodoxy holds that these are the only two possibilities. Sowell rejects them both on the grounds that they are rationalistic constructs that abstract from the complex of concrete contingencies and relativities that produce the statistical disparities in question.

Sowell asserts that the civil rights vision "is not only a moral vision of the way the world *should* be in the future, but also a cause-and-effect vision of the way the world *is* today." [297] There are three central and particularly controversial premises at the heart of the civil rights vision that he mentions, but for the moment, I want to focus only on two of them. The first is that "statistical disparities in incomes, occupations, education, etc., represent moral inequities, and are caused by 'society.'" [298] The second is that "belief in innate inferiority explains policies and practices of differential treatment, whether expressed in overt hostility or in institutional policies or individual decisions that result in statistical disparities." Sowell writes:

> *Ironically, the innate inferiority doctrine and the opposite "equal representation" doctrine proceed on the same intellectual premise—that one can go from innate ability to observed result without major concern for intervening cultural factors. Unexplained residual differences between groups, after controlling for such gross differences as education or parental income, are attributed by one vision to discrimination and by the other to genetics.*

He concludes that:

> *...there are apparently no other reasons for differences in skill or capability other than discrimination, which is illegal, or innate inferiority, which is rejected. Or so it appears in the civil rights vision.*[299]

Neither the prevailing racial orthodoxy nor the much less popular doctrine of innate inferiority is adequate to account for inter-racial inequalities. In stark contrast to these abstract approaches, Sowell's conservative study situates the inequalities that obtain between white and black Americans within an expansive context that is at once historical and international. Let us turn to the first principle of the civil rights vision: discrimination is the inevitable culprit of statistical disparities between racial groups.

Before critiquing it, Sowell notes that this principle implicitly relies upon at least three presuppositions that, though perhaps plausible, are nevertheless demonstrably false.

The first, and apparently most obvious, is that discrimination leads to adverse effects on the observable achievements of those who are discriminated against, as compared to the discriminators or to society in general. The second assumption is that the converse of this is equally true—that statistical differences signal, imply and/or measure discrimination. This assumption depends upon a third unspoken premise—that large statistical differences between groups do not usually arise and persist without discrimination.

This last assumption must figure in the civil rights vision, Sowell remarks, for if substantial statistical disparities between groups can occur in the absence of discrimination, "then discrimination takes its place as only one cause among many—and inferences from statistical disparities lose their validity as evidence." This state of affairs would in no way disprove the existence of discrimination, but it would undermine "the convenient statistical barometer..."[300]

In truth, though, "statistical disparities are commonplace among human beings," a fact for which there are "many historical and cultural reasons..."[301] The Chinese in southeast Asia, Jews in numerous societies throughout the world, East Indians in Africa, southeast Asia, and various areas in the western hemisphere, Italians in South America, and the Japanese in the United States are among some of the racial groups that have *flourished* in the midst of being systematically discriminated against by the majority populations with which they have had to co-exist. The Chinese, for example, "for several centuries" in southeast Asia, "has been—and continues to be—the target of explicit, legalized discrimination in various occupations, in admission to institutions of higher learning, and suffers bans and restrictions on land ownership and places of residence." Still, in Malaysia, Indonesia, Vietnam, Thailand, and the Philippines, the Chinese, who constitute no more than 5% of the population of all of Southeast Asia, "owns a majority of the nation's total investments in key industries."[302] In spite of the fact that they "encountered persistent and escalating discrimination, culminating in their mass internment during World War II," the Japanese in the United States, by as early as 1959, "had about equaled the income of whites," and a decade later, "Japanese American families were earning nearly one-third higher incomes than the average American family." [303]

Sowell concedes that given the unique history of blacks in America, black Americans are a "special case." However, he argues that even the history and circumstances of this group defy the principle in question. In Latin America, blacks "have not been subjected to as rigid and severe segregation, oppression, or violence as blacks in the United States. Yet blacks in Brazil...are economically *farther behind* whites than are blacks in the United States...." [304] Furthermore, while slavery is among the most invidious forms of discrimination, and in spite of the frequency with which "the legacy of slavery" argument is made to account for the assortment of pathologies found among contemporary black Americans, Sowell points out that the evidence undermines this argument. With respect to the high illegitimacy rate and number of single parent headed households among black Americans, Sowell remarks: "Most black children, even under slavery, grew up in two-parent households. A teenage girl raising a child with no man present was a rarity among blacks, both during the era of slavery and as late as the 1920's." [305]

Crime is another issue. "Few people today are aware that the ghettos in many cities were far safer places just two generations ago [Sowell wrote this in 1984] than they are today, both for blacks and whites." Sowell notes that "incredulity often greets stories by older blacks as to their habit of sleeping out on fire escapes or on rooftops or in public parks on hot summer nights. Many of those same people would not dare to walk through those same parks today in broad daylight." [306]

It was not uncommon for whites in the 1930's, believe it or not, to regularly spend evenings in Harlem, often not leaving until late morning hours, when they would hail taxis to drive them to their homes. "Today," Sowell observes, "not only would very few whites dare to do this, very few cabs would dare to be cruising ghetto streets in the wee hours of the morning." He asks rhetorically:

> *If crime is a product of poverty and discrimination as they [proponents of the civil rights vision] say endlessly, why was there so much less of it when poverty and discrimination were much worse than today? If massive programs are the only hope to reduce violence in the ghetto, why was there so much less violence long before anyone ever thought of these programs?*[307]

Statistical comparisons between "blacks" and "whites," Sowell observes, trade in interpersonal abstractions as opposed to flesh and blood persons. Each group consists of several subgroups, some of which have virtually nothing but skin color in common with the others with which they are conflated.

Take West Indians, for instance. West Indians are biologically indistinguishable from American blacks, yet by nearly every social index the two groups are as different from one another as are "blacks" and "whites." In *Ethnic America,* Sowell attributes this to the difference in conduct between these two groups. "West Indians were much more frugal, hard-working, and entrepreneurial [than American blacks]. Their children worked harder and outperformed native black children in school," and they "had lower fertility rates and lower crime rates than either black or white Americans."[308] In *The Economics and Politics of Race,* Sowell elaborates further, telling us that as far back as 1969, West Indian blacks in America earned 94% of the average income of Americans generally, as opposed to American blacks, who earned but 62%, and second-generation West Indians "earned 15 percent *more* than the average American." [309] Sowell's point is that the experience of West Indians in America reveals that the appeal to discrimination in accounting for black-white inequalities is not only not the foregone conclusion that it is often taken to be, but fails even as an hypothesis, for white racism should prevent both types of blacks from succeeding, given that to a white racist, "all blacks look alike."

However, even focusing on American blacks alone we immediately discover that they comprise anything but a monolithic group. Sowell says that marriage, age, education, and region of residence are just some of the factors that are crucial in determining a range of social phenomena.

As of nearly a half-a-century ago, black males who came from homes where there were newspapers, magazines, and library cards had the same incomes as whites from similar homes and with the same numbers of years of schooling. In the 1970's, black husband-and wife families outside the South earned as much as white husband-and-wife families outside the South. By 1981, for the country as a whole, black husband-and-wife families where both were college educated and both working earned slightly *more* than white families of the same description. [310]

Sowell concludes:

> *Many of the "racial" differences based on gross statistics are shown by a finer breakdown to be differences between people with different values and lifestyles, who are differing proportions of different racial populations. Where the values and lifestyles are comparable, the economic and social outcomes have tended to be comparable.* [311]

The second premise of the civil rights vision—that assumption that discrimination must be due to a belief in innate inferiority on the part of the discriminators—is just as dubious as the first. Sowell remarks that not only is it the case that "many of the groups most subject to violence have not been generally viewed as innately inferior," but, in fact, they "have been hated precisely because of [their] superior performances as economic competitors." Chinese, East Indians, Jews, and Armenians are some of the examples that Sowell cites. He does not deny that the doctrine of innate inferiority has indeed often accompanied the discrimination that has been exercised against black Americans historically, yet he notes that such discrimination does not, as the civil rights vision supposes, necessarily result from a belief in innate inferiority. "Even the enslavement of blacks," Sowell says, "was not the result of a doctrine of innate inferiority." Rather, "this doctrine developed as a rationalization of slavery" after the institution came under increasing criticism in the West, and after "religious rationalizations—enslaving 'heathens' for their own spiritual good—were first used and then abandoned as more slaves became Christians…" [312]

Sowell sums up, saying:

> …belief in the innate inferiority doctrine has been neither necessary nor sufficient to explain intergroup hostility, oppression, violence, or enslavement. [313]

The third proposition central to the civil rights vision is that it is primarily, if not exclusively, through political activity that "underrepresented" groups are to advance. This is the quintessential rationalist assumption that "social engineering" is desirable. Sowell challenges it, saying that all of the empirical evidence shows that political power is "neither necessary nor sufficient for economic advancement. Nor has eager political participation or outstanding success in politics been translated into faster group achievement." [314]

The Chinese in Southeast Asia, the Caribbean, and the United States; the Germans in Brazil, Australia, and the United

States; the English in Argentina; the Jews in America, Britain, and South Africa; and the Italians in America and Argentina are among the various groups of people who have prospered economically and socially while steadfastly refusing to participate in politics. [315] While the Irish *did* advance through politics, "their rise from poverty was much *slower* than that of other groups who were nowhere near being their political equals," and in spite of the presence of Irish political machines in many large American cities in the latter part of the nineteenth century, "the great bulk of the Irish populace remained unskilled laborers and domestic servants...." Irish-American citizens didn't start to achieve economic prosperity until many years later, when the Irish political machinery began to wane. [316]

In *Black Rednecks and White Liberals,* Sowell looks at the black American experience. "The civil rights legislation of the 1960's," he says, "may well have been an *effect* of the rise of blacks, rather than the sole or predominant cause of that rise..." That so many of us believe otherwise, Sowell explains, is due to the fact black and white "civil rights leaders," motivated by the need "to magnify their own role in racial progress," have labored tirelessly to impress this idea into the popular consciousness. [317] He notes that while...

> ...the Civil Rights Act of 1964 and the Voting Rights Act of 1965 dealt major blows to racial restrictions...and had dramatic effects on the number of black elected officials [economically speaking,] the upward trends in black income and occupations that had begun decades earlier simply continued, but at no accelerated rate. [318]

Furthermore, "the rise of blacks into professional and other high-level occupations was...greater in the years *preceding* the Civil Rights Act of 1964 than in the years afterward, and was greater in the 1940's than in the 1950's."[319] For example, 87% of black families were living in poverty in 1940. By 1960, before the historic civil rights legislation that was to follow a few years later, this rate had fallen to 47%. Although beset by periods of retrogression in race relations—e.g., the post-Reconstruction era in the South, and the imposition of rigid racial restrictions on Northern blacks following the mass migrations of Southern blacks to the North before World War I—black Americans made remarkable economic and educational advances every decade from emancipation onward, but *the rate* at which such advances occurred were greater before 1960 than afterward.

Sowell's position on the role of politics in society is reflective of his conservatism. Like other conservatives, he views politics as the limited activity of governing, of preserving the legal conditions without which an orderly society is impossible. But the politics of the conservative is what has elsewhere been called "the politics of skepticism."[320] Conservatives, as we have seen, have little sympathy for the idea that government should direct society in the pursuit of some great enterprise or other, for they hold that in a genuinely *civil* society, whose members are associated to one another in terms of laws that extend equally to all, there is no grand enterprise that can engage the attention and energies of every citizen. It is the model of war, conservatives believe, that is the inspiration for rationalists of all stripes who are determined to transform society into some awesome enterprise association or another, for it is in times of war when the resources of citizens are conscripted and enlisted in the service of an ideal or set of ideals, and it is during such times especially when individuality and plurality pose the gravest threat.

On the issue of black progress, Sowell claims that "the economic advancement of blacks, both absolutely and relative to whites…was due to the individual efforts of millions of black people trying to better their own lives."[321] Blacks were able to flourish "under the most adverse conditions" because of those "little platoons" like family, church, and local community—virtue forming institutions intermediate between the individual and the State that were the products of their cultural tradition. Not only did law do little to facilitate their substantial social gains, it was not infrequently antagonistic to the social well-being of black Americans.

Moreover, Sowell doesn't think that, generally speaking, anyhow, government *can* achieve substantive satisfactions like equality or the elimination of racism without creating problems at least as great, and usually greater, than those with which it is concerned. Whereas "crusaders like to talk about 'solutions,'" in reality "life is actually one trade-off after another." In the final resort, there is but one fundamental question that is the concern of politics: "What are you prepared to give up in order to get what you want?" [322] With respect to "affirmative action," Sowell explains that by overlooking a number of factors, such as differences in age and geographical preference between demographic and racial groups, and attributing the lack of "proportional representation" to discrimination, its proponents have unwittingly *harmed* the very people whose interests they claim to champion. "Affirmative action" creates special rights that are "costs to the recipients themselves." He writes:

The general unattainability of many quotas means that penalties fall equally on discriminatory employers and nondiscriminatory employers. A discriminatory employer therefore has little to gain by becoming a nondiscriminatory employer, when the characteristics of the target population (age, education, etc.) insure that he will be unable to fill quotas anyway.

Furthermore:

> ...the ease with which a discrimination case can be made makes minorities and women more dangerous employees to have, in terms of

> *future prospects of law suits if their subsequent pay, promotions, or other benefits do not match those of other employees or the expectations of administrative agencies.*[323]

There are two other types of cost that preferential treatment policies impose. They increase social tensions and result in a loss of freedom. In *Is Reality Optional?*, Sowell says that preferential treatment policies, what is referred to as "affirmative action" in the United States, have been practiced in a wide range of countries, from Nigeria to Sri Lanka to New Zealand. In spite of the vast differences between these societies, as well as the differences between the groups who are the recipients of preferential treatment, there are numerous resemblances, the most pervasive of which is the "polarization" that preferential treatment policies produce. In those places where these policies have been in place for longest, like India and Sri Lanka, the social strife has translated into bloodshed.[324]

There are two ways that "affirmative action" imperils freedom, according to Sowell. For one, the usurpation of heterogeneity through the imposition of homogeneity that it entails necessarily requires an expansion of governmental power and a corresponding loss of freedom on the part of individuals to make their own hiring decisions. Sowell writes:

> *Much focus on the desirability of the various outcomes being sought distracts attentions from the fundamental change of processes required to pursue those outcomes. Metaphors about how "society" should "arrange" this or that result evade the institutional reality that someone must be empowered to constrict other people's freedom—and thus evade the need to weigh whether the expected value of the result being sought, given the chances of achieving*

> *it, is greater or less than the expected value of the loss of freedom that this effort entails* [325]

The other sense in which freedom is undermined by "affirmative action" concerns the rule of law, which requires that all laws be known or at least knowable in advance of our actions. Yet discrimination, when conceived against the backdrop of affirmative action laws, can have no "clear prospective meaning, such as applying different standards to members of different groups or subjecting some to more onerous processes than others," but "must be defined by retrospective results, whether 'disparate impact' or 'hostile environments'..." Attempts to bring to fruition "equal results or equal prospects, with little or no regard for whether the individuals or groups involved are in equal circumstances or have equal capabilities or equal personal drives," frustrates that mechanism without which a free society, or, for that matter, any stable society, is impossible: the rule of law. Methods to secure substantive equality:

> *...cannot operate under general rules, the essence of law, but must create categories of people entitled to various outcomes, regardless of their own inputs.* [326]

Conclusion

In this chapter, by focusing on the writings of Thomas Sowell, a thinker widely acknowledged by both friends and foes as the most articulate of voices of "black conservatism," and, quite possibly, the chief inspiration for the school of thought so-called, I hoped to show that, in reality, "black conservatism" is a fiction, for Sowell speaks from an intellectual tradition, not of *black* conservatism, but of conservatism, a tradition that spans over two centuries and whose most notable representatives have not been black. Sowell rejects the liberal rationalism of the civil rights vision on issues concerning race, preferring instead to focus on both this vision and the issues from a conservative perspective. Neither does this, though, suffice to establish that he is a "black conservative," for non-black conservatives have done the same. His conservative critique of the civil rights vision, itself a variant of an enlightenment liberal tradition at least as old as conservatism, does, however, clarify why Sowell—a black thinker—is regarded, especially by his opponents, as a "black conservative."

Chapter 6

CONSERVATISM and RACE: THE PHILOSOPHY OF "BLACK CONSERVATIVE" GEORGE S. SCHUYLER

Introduction

FOR HIS PRODIGIOUS efforts in assembling the essays of forgotten "black conservative" George Samuel Schuyler, as well as for his recognition of the latter's considerable talents in his capacities as both writer and thinker, Jeffrey B. Leak deserves much credit.[327] Leak does not share the political and philosophical predilections of the subject of his study, a fact that reveals his treatment of Schuyler to be that much more commendable. This praise aside, though, Leak's own ideological biases conspire with an all too typically provincial focus on American intellectual and political life to *reinforce* the very prejudices against the "black conservatism" represented by the likes of Schuyler that Leak presumably set out to dispel.

While acknowledging Schuyler's adeptness at dealing with race-related issues throughout his long and illustrious career, Leak simultaneously criticizes him for "his unshakable commitment at times to the most extreme forms of conservatism," [328] "the political far right" or "radical conservatism," [329] a commitment that rendered him vulnerable to the charge—articulated by, among others, the distinguished black historian, E. Franklin Frazier—that Schuyler was a "race traitor." [330] Although Leak refuses to endorse this allegation, and although he agrees with Cornel West[331] that conservatives like Schuyler are correct in rejecting "blind" loyalty to race, he also concurs with West's verdict that black conservatives tend to substitute for "blind loyalty to the race" a "blind loyalty to the nation." Schuyler, in Leak's estimation, was particularly guilty of this as he devoted his energies toward "extreme forms of conservative idealism rather than racial justice." [332] Schuyler's "conservative ideology" became increasingly "uncompassionate," "reactionary," and "insensitive and misguided;" [333] it embodied an "excess" [334] of "regrettable polemics" [335] and a profoundly "compromised....critical sensibility." [336]

Leak is mistaken. In what follows, I argue that while Schuyler was indeed a conservative, he was not the reactionary ideologue of Leaks' imagination. Rather, Schuyler drew upon the resources of a rich, and richly heterogeneous, centuries-old European intellectual tradition now widely regarded as "conservatism." And he drew upon it in order to combat what he perceived to be the folly, not of "black liberalism," but of that of his opponents' *rationalism,* another specifically European intellectual tradition with roots stretching back even further than the conservatism that it initially elicited as a response. The version of rationalism upon which Schuyler set his sights is what I have chosen to call "Blackism," an ideology that purports to supply the key to "racial authenticity"—and which he believed threatened to undermine racial harmony.

This paper is divided into four sections. In the first, I provide a summary of rationalism, and in the second, the principles of Blackism are delineated. The third section is reserved for a summary of conservatism, while the fourth is an exposition of Schuyler's location within this tradition.

Rationalism

Rationalism has assumed many forms over its extensive and varied life. Yet while it is not inappropriate to speak of multiple rationalism*s*, each is related to all of the others by way of a set of commonly shared philosophical presuppositions—epistemological, ethical, and political-philosophical—on account of which rationalism is the distinctive tradition that it is.

Reason and Knowledge

In Michael Oakeshott's perceptive exposition of rationalism, he notes that the latter springs from a peculiar conception of knowledge. Knowledge is of two kinds, "technical" and "practical," or "traditional," Oakeshott writes. Although every conceivable activity encompasses both, the proponent of rationalism tends to identify the whole of knowledge with technical knowledge. The latter has the advantage, or at least appears to have the advantage, over traditional knowledge in that, being "susceptible of formulation in rules, principles, directions, maxims—comprehensively, in propositions," it conveys "at least the appearance of certainty...." [337] "Technical knowledge," Oakeshott continues, "can be learned from a book" or "a correspondence course"; in other words, "it can be learned by heart, repeated by rote, and applied mechanically...." Simply put, technical knowledge "can be both taught and learned in the simplest meanings of these words." [338]

In glaring contrast, traditional knowledge "exists only in use, is not reflective and (unlike technique) cannot be formulated in rules." [339] The "normal expression" of practical or traditional knowledge is located "in a customary or traditional way of doing things...." This, in turn, "gives it the appearance of imprecision and consequently of uncertainty, of being a matter of opinion, of probability rather than truth."

This kind of knowledge lacks "rigidity." It "can neither be taught nor learned, but only imparted and acquired" through "practice." [340]

For the rationalist, technical knowledge is synonymous with knowledge itself. In conceiving knowledge as a *technique,* the rationalist opts for an "ideology" over a tradition of conduct, and he makes this choice because of the ideology's "greater precision and its alleged demonstrability," [341] "its appearance of being self-contained." [342] An ideology or technique conveys "the appearance of *certainty.*" [343]

Ethics & Political Philosophy

Inseparable from the rationalist's epistemic vision is his vision of political-morality. "The morality of the Rationalist is the morality of the self-conscious pursuit of moral ideals" and the "moral education" that he prefers assumes the form of "the presentation and explanation of moral principles" [344]—like the principles of "natural" or "human rights" found in the Declaration of Independence.[345] The principles-centered morality of rationalism is an *ideology* or technique, more specifically, "the morality of the self-made man and the self-made society...." [346]

As far as politics are concerned, the rationalist's penchant is for "destruction and creation"—*not* "acceptance or reform." This is because either by design or through inadvertence, he equates change with that which is "self-consciously induced...." As a result, he identifies "the customary and the traditional with the changeless." [347]

This conception of change, coupled with his desire to bring it about, conspire to engender the rationalist's faith in both the possibility of "an innocuous power which may safely be made so great as to be able to control all other powers in the human world," as well as his confidence "that political machinery can take the place of moral and political education." [348] It isn't necessarily the case that the thought of the rationalist is "governed in each occasion by a comprehensive utopia;" however, the rationalist is "invariably...a perfectionist in detail." [349] Examples of the rationalist's political philosophy abound. The idea that whole societies can be erected upon "a Declaration of the Rights of Man," is one. Others are notions of such "universal principles" as "national" or "racial self-determination...." [350]

Blackism

Like all ideologies, what I refer to as "Blackism" is what Oakeshott described as a *technique*. And as is the case with all ideologies, the knowledge that it purports to provide is comprised of propositions with which anyone can become familiar. However, while anyone, in theory, can confine the tenets of Blackism to memory, *only* a person who is biologically *black* can *become* a Blackist. Being racially or biologically black—to *any* extent—is a *necessary* condition that must be met before one can become a proponent of Blackism, but it is also sufficient—as long as one affirms the principles of Blackism. What this means is that subscription to Blackism does *not* require fluency in black *culture*. In fact, it is not a stretch to say that it is a contrivance for which precisely those blacks who crave racial "authenticity" but who have not immersed themselves in black culture are the principal beneficiaries. This being said, there most certainly is a relationship between black culture and Blackism, yet it is the same relationship that exists between any ideology and the tradition or practice of which it is the distillation: Blackism stands in relation to black culture as a set of cliff notes stands in relation to the text of which it is the abridgment. Blackism draws from aspects of black culture or "the black experience" in America, but, like the caricature that it is, it wildly distorts the dimensions to which it speaks.

So, what is Blackism? The ideology of Blackism is distinguished on account of five mutually supplementary features, principles, or themes. This list of features is more impressionistic than exhaustive, and Blackists may and do disagree as to which warrant greatest emphasis. However, consideration of Blackism brings to light the following.

The first is the linchpin of its worldview: the Blackist's racialized conception of history. On this conception, historical actors are abstract racial categories—whites, blacks, etc.—and history itself is a melodramatic contest between the forces of "white racism" or "white supremacy," on the one hand, and "the oppression" suffered by "people of color," on the other. It is not a stretch to characterize Blackist "history" as a species of solipsism, for in spite of the nods that it occasionally gives in the way of black suffering in other parts of the world, it largely coalesces around a truncated vision of the *American* past and present: time essentially begins and ends within the American mind.

The second principle of Blackism, clearly rooted in the first, is the belief in the endemic character of "white racism." Some Blackists attribute the ills of blacks almost solely to "white racism," while others refuse to go quite that far. Some Blackists think that not only hasn't "white racism" diminished over the decades, it has actually grown more threatening; others claim to recognize that while "white racism" remains "potent," it has abated. Still, these degrees in understanding aside, all Blackists affirm—and must affirm—that "white racism" always has been and remains a genuine obstacle to black flourishing.

Third, the Blackist must never fail to give expression to some measure of indignation or rage regarding the near omnipresence of "white racism."

Fourth, the Blackist must be an unabashed champion of "social" or "racial justice." That is, he must not only support above and beyond all else the advancement of blacks; he must esteem as the most pivotal instrument toward this end a robust, activist federal government.

Finally, integral to Blackism is the notion of "racial

authenticity." Racial authenticity—authentic blackness—requires nothing more or less than affirmation, *by a biologically black person,* of the tenets of Blackism.

If Blackism can be said to have a "High Priest," a quintessential spokesperson, it would be Malcolm X. Malcolm spent the overwhelming majority of his public career as a national minister for the Nation of Islam—a black supremacist cult deemed illegitimate by the Islamic world—condemning all whites as "devils." During his time with the Nation, as well as afterwards, Malcolm personified each of Blackism's tenets.

Malcolm would invoke "the authority of history" as he condemned whites for their transgressions against blacks and others. Whites, he charged, "stole our fathers and mothers from their culture of silk and satins and brought them to this land in the belly of a ship...." Ever since, "this blue-eyed devil" whose "time has about to run out" "has kept us in chains...." [351] Black people "didn't land on Plymouth Rock," Malcolm once said, but "Plymouth Rock landed" on blacks.[352] American blacks—"twenty-two million black men"—have invested in their country, or been made to invest in it, "four hundred years of toil"—and yet "they are still today at the bottom of everything!" [353] The white race has "thrust" itself "into the position of leadership in the world" by way of "the use of naked physical power," through "conquering, killing, exploiting, pillaging, raping, bullying," and "beating." Throughout "his entire advance through history, he has been waving the banner of Christianity" in the one hand and, in the other, "the sword and the flintlock." [354]

Malcolm not only reliably—inexhaustibly—drew upon his racialized "history" while expressing indignation over "white racism;" he also spared no occasion to assert his own racial authenticity while condemning other blacks as inauthentic. In *Malcolm: The Life of a Man Who Changed Black America,* Bruce Perry writes:

He [Malcolm] characterized Booker T. Washington as a "white man's nigger" and lampooned the NAACP as a "black body with a white head." Even Jackie Robinson and Joe Louis, whom he had idolized, were "stooges" for the white establishment....And despite his reluctant admiration for Martin Luther King, Jr., he portrayed him as a "chump, not a champ".....

Malcolm, Perry notes, described black proponents of integration as "'Quislings' and 'Uncle Toms.'" He charged them with desiring "'white skins,'" depicted them "as blacks with white hearts," and lambasted them "for living in white neighborhoods and for being dependent on white money." Malcolm even referred to those activists who endured beatings at the hands of police officers as "'masochists.'" [355] The likes of Martin Luther King, Jr. and Roy Wilkins Malcolm ridiculed as "modern house Negroes" and "Toms." [356]

It is true that upon being exiled from the Nation of Islam, Malcolm claimed to have rejected "racism." Yet while he abandoned "the white devil" and "Uncle Tom" rhetoric of his past, his efforts to have the United States tried and convicted by the United Nations on the charge that it was guilty of violating "the human rights" of its black citizens, as well as his related aim to extract reparations for American blacks,[357] establish definitively that Malcolm's Blackist vision remained fully intact.

The ideology of Blackism *is* the dominant ideology of the contemporary black intelligentsia. The most random selection of black-authored literature readily reveals this. Take, for instance, the notable academic, Cornel West. West correctly observes in the very first line of his discussion of "Identity and Race" in the fourth chapter of his *Hope on a Tightrope:* "We have to get our stories right from the very beginning," for "any discussion of race has to do with how we tell the story." [358] From the Blackist's perspective, the story is the "244 years" that "black folk had no legal status, no social standing, no public worth whatever...." [359] It consists in "244 years of white supremacist slavery, 87 years of white supremacist Jim and Jane Crow, and then another 40 years in which significant progress has been made." What this means is that since "stereotypes still cut deep," whites who want to affirm "the humanity" of blacks and other non-whites "must undergo a kind of conversion, metamorphosis, and transformation." [360] Nothing less than "transformation" on the part of whites is needed because, "for the West," the idea "that black people are human beings" is "a revolutionary concept." [361]

In keeping with Blackism's narrative of unrelenting "white supremacy," West remarks that *this* is "the real original sin" of America in which "African oppression" is grounded. White supremacy is "the precondition for a nation that could then be founded on the exploitation, subjugation, and hatred of African people." [362] It is "the white supremacy inside of black people" that "leads us to demean ourselves and devalue ourselves." [363]

As for the notions of racial *authenticity* and "social justice," West is to the point: "'Black enough' always means 'bold enough.'" He elaborates: "Clarence Thomas," for instance, "is phenotypically, beautifully black." However, as "a right-wing conservative who sides with the strong against the weak," Thomas is "not bold enough."

Thus, he is most definitely *not* black enough.[364]

In stark contrast, take Thurgood Marshall and Adam Clayton Powell. "Thurgood Marshall was a beautiful high-yellow black." But "he was black enough because he was bold enough. He didn't side with the strong, he sided with the weak." Powell "looked like a Puerto Rican," but blacks "loved him. How come? He was bold enough, which made him black enough." [365] Of course, being "bold enough" means sparing no occasion to advance the cause of black liberation or "social justice."

To put it another way, being "bold enough," being "black enough," means affirming Blackism.

Conservatism

If rationalism can be said to have a nemesis, it is that orientation that has come to acquire the name of "conservatism." In fact, given its endorsement of epistemological, ethical, and political philosophical conceptions that are antithetical to those espoused by rationalism, modern conservatism emerged as *the* response to the rationalistic excesses of Enlightenment.

Reason & Knowledge

In his *Reflections on the Revolution in France,* Edmund Burke supplied for all subsequent generations as clear a statement of the conservative's reservations concerning reason as any that has been provided. Burke writes:

> *We are afraid to put men to live and trade each on his own private stock of reason; because we suspect that this stock in each man is small, and that individuals would be better to avail themselves of the general bank and capital of nations, and of ages.* [366]

Burke articulates what some commentators have described as an epistemology grounded in "modesty." [367] He commends England's "men of speculation" on their resolve to desist from the enterprise of "exploding general prejudices" while using "their sagacity to discover the latent wisdom which prevails in them." [368] Upon examining these perennial prejudices, the wise opt for "the prejudice, with the reason involved," over "the naked reason," for the former "has a motive to give action to that reason, and an affection that will give it permanence." [369]

On this conception, reason is constituted by the constraints of cultural tradition. While neither Burke nor any other conservative would deny that reason has access to "principles" or propositions, unlike rationalists, they recognize that knowledge is not only "technical," but "traditional," as Oakeshott describes it. Traditional knowledge "exists only in use;" it "is not reflective;" and it differs from technical knowledge in that it defies explicit formulation in propositional terms.[370]

Morality and Political Philosophy

The moral and political philosophies of the rationalist embody a universal and impartial perspective. They invariably consist of propositions, usually "principles" and/or "ideals," that are allegedly independent of any and every cultural and historical contingency. More often than not, these principles are held to specify "natural" or "human rights."

The conservative rejects this vision. The principles of an ideology are not timeless verities, but the abridgements of culturally-specifically traditions. "Circumstances," Burke declares, "give in reality to every political principle its distinguishing color and discriminating effect." It is "circumstances" that "render every civil and political scheme beneficial or noxious to mankind." [371] The problem with the rationalist's doctrine of "the rights of men" is the same problem that confronts all ideologies: an ideology is inflexible because its claims are categorical. "Against these [the rights of men] there can be no prescription; against these no argument is binding." The doctrine of "the rights of men" defy "temperament" and "compromise...." [372]

Burke insists upon an inverse relationship between the cogency of *the metaphysics* of the rationalist and that of his *political-morality*. "The pretended rights of these theorists," he remarks, "are all extremes; and in proportion as they are metaphysically true, they are morally and politically false." [373] The "abstract perfection" of "the rights of men" is "their practical defect." In reality, our "liberties...vary with times and circumstances, and admit of infinite modifications"—a fact that precludes all attempts to establish them upon the "principle" of an "abstract rule." [374] Whatever sense there may (or may not) be in discussing "the original rights of man," it is "the civil social man, and no other," with which we concern ourselves in politics. Rights, thus, "is a thing "to be settled by convention." [375] The conservative tradition to which Burke gave rise is antithetical to modern rationalism. Epistemologically, ethically, and political-philosophically, it affirms precisely those tradition-centered conceptions of reason, morality, and the state that rationalism resolutely rejects. We will now see that George Schuyler falls squarely within this tradition.

George S. Schuyler

George Schuyler was quite possibly among the greatest editorialists that America ever produced. Born in 1895 in Rhode Island, Schuyler lived in Syracuse, New York with his family until he was old enough to enlist in the United States Army. Upon the completion of World War I, he returned to civilian life, taking up residence in Harlem, where he remained until his death in 1977. It was during the decade of the 1920's when, from a thirst for intellectual stimulation rather than the appeal of its ideas, Schuyler joined the Socialist Party and began to travel within circles that would subsequently be identified with "the Harlem Renaissance." It was also during this decade that he began establishing for himself a rapidly expanding reputation as a writer. Throughout his life, in addition to authoring what has been called the first black science fiction novel, *Black No More,* Schuyler wrote as well for a plethora of other publications, black and white, including *American Mercury,* founded and edited by H.L. Mencken, the largest of literary giants of that time. Schuyler was a tireless champion for racial equality and a vehement opponent of communism. From 1922 until 1964, he was the editor for *The Pittsburg Courier,* the largest black newspaper publication in the country. In 1966, Schuyler composed his autobiography, *Black and Conservative*.[376]

If Malcolm X's can be said to be the quintessential voice of Blackism, then it is with no small measure of justice that we can say of Schuyler's that his is the voice of "anti-Blackism." In fact, on more than one occasion, Schuyler and Malcolm X faced off—with results that a remotely unprejudiced observer could only characterize as devastating for the latter.

During one round table radio discussion on "The Black Muslims in America" that transpired while Malcolm was still a member of The Nation of Islam, Schuyler pulled no punches.—neither with Malcolm, nor his other interlocutors.[377] But given the topic of the exchange, it was primarily upon Malcolm that he set his sights.

Given his first opportunity to speak, Schuyler brilliantly and decisively laid waste to the ideology of Blackism espoused by Malcolm and The Nation of Islam. Its "anti-Christian" and "anti-white" character, Schuyler began, is rooted in the erroneous belief "that white Christians were responsible for slavery in the world...." However, "this is one of the many falsehoods upon which this movement [The Nation] is founded," for it was "the Moslems" who "carried on slavery" for centuries upon centuries "before the white European Christians started it." [378]

American blacks, Schuyler indignantly remarked, are "the healthiest" and "the wealthiest" blacks in the world. They "have the most property" and they are "the best educated" and "the best informed group of Negroes" on the planet—"*and that includes all those in the Muslim countries.*" [379]

Throughout this conversation on the Black Muslims—as throughout his life—Schuyler continually repudiated the rationalist abstractionism of his Blackist opponents while remaining rooted in the empiricism characteristic of his conservatism. Urging Malcolm to return to "the field of reality," he pointed out to him that his claim that blacks are excluded from the country's economy is simply absurd on its

117

face. Blacks buy and sell like everyone else, and in the case of a couple of hundred thousand black farmers particularly, they do much of the selling to whites. They are members of labor unions, not infrequently holding some of the highest positions. Malcolm's assertions to the contrary aside, they are *not,* "necessarily," "the last ones hired, first ones fired." [380] And even if it is true that the black unemployment rate is higher than that among whites, it is illegitimate to argue from this statistic to the conclusion that *it is because they are "Negro"* that blacks have higher rates of unemployment.[381]

The racial collectivities on which the Blackist's "history" depends simply—and abysmally—fail to do justice to the intricacies and nuances that an empirical consideration of reality reveals. In reality, while blacks, not unlike every other group of people that have ever existed, have indeed had to endure slavery and racial oppression, it is no less true that whites have gone to great lengths to assist blacks, both in America as well as elsewhere, in improving their condition. "If," Schuyler asked, "the white man has hated the Negro since he has been on the earth, why has the white man done so much to help the Negro?" Whites, for instance, "abolished the slave trade in Africa and from here to Africa...." Not a single Islamic state can claim to have done the same. Furthermore, whites have "set up schools and clinics and hospitals and asylums and colleges throughout all black Africa," yet "I don't know whether anybody can point out one Moslem college or university south of Egypt and Morocco in Africa" that has been established "for the education of black people." There are certainly whites who hate blacks, but the ideology of Blackism represented by the likes of Malcolm, like all rationalist abstractions, reduces the complexity of human experience and individuality to categorical simplicities.[382]

The poverty of nuance from which the ideological "history" of the Blackist suffers is evident not only in its glaring omission of the fact that slavery was being practiced in Africa by non-white Muslims for centuries and centuries before the first white Christian ever stepped foot on the Dark Continent. It is also reflected by its neglect of the inconvenient facts that, first, by every conventional social indicia, American blacks are far better off than the vast majority of people—of any color—who have ever lived; and, second, whites have labored, and continue to labor, indefatigably to aid blacks in America and Africa. The Blackist's ahistorical racial narrative also ignores the reality of *the enslavement of whites* generally and, specifically, the enslavement of whites *in early America.*

Schuyler correctly notes that it was not at all "unusual for unmixed Nordics [whites] to be sold into servitude, either in America or elsewhere." If whites in bondage "could not be sold on the wharves in Boston, New York or Philadelphia, they were marched manacled through the countryside to be sold to farmers for the passage money due the captain." Schuyler remarks upon the unbalanced coverage of black and white slavery, respectively:

It is the custom to illustrate every book on the slave trade with a picture of the manner in which the [African] slaves were packed into the holds. What is rarely shown is the manner in which European servants were similarly packed in like sardines, often with lower ceilings than the slave ships had.[383]

All of this, of course, is absent from the Blackist's racialized melodrama of White Oppression and Black Suffering.

Blackism, Schuyler believed, all too easily shaded into racism. As one who spent his entire life combating "the majority [white] attitude" toward blacks, an attitude that he describes as "morally wrong, nonsensical, unfair, un-Christian and cruelly unjust,"[384] Schuyler found this deeply disturbing. In "The Rising Tide of Black Racism," he writes that Negroes were now in the process of acquiring the "racial fictions" of whites. "Having lugubriously wailed for generations over the cruelty of the color bar and the panting of the prideful so-called Aryans," Schuyler notes, black activists "more and more sound like the White Citizens Council agitators of yesteryear."

[385] With alarming frequency, race is enlisted in the service of excusing "moral dereliction" and criminality[386] as black "preachers…convert their pulpits into agitator's soapboxes spewing rabid racism…."

More disconcerting is that "this racist self-serving" is becoming ever more prevalent just as white racism appears to be on the wane. "The meanest motives have been attributed to all white people indiscriminately," he comments, "at the most promising period in race relations in our national history." Black activists exaggerate "every distemper…into an epidemic while white-dominated legislatures" are busy passing "numerous civil rights laws in excess of anything previously known" and "opportunities for education and employment unprecedented for Negro youth" are made available. Black "agitators" trade off "moderation and compromise, the essence of statesmanship," in favor of "self-denigration, absurd demands for preference, and unbecoming racial truculence…." This phenomenon poses "a real, present, and future danger" to the country, for in seeing "much-touted leaders rushing to cover up delinquency, immorality and crimes because the perpetrators are colored," black youth, rather than "think in terms of individual excellence," are likely to have their heads "contaminated by a cloud of racist propaganda." [387]

In principle, the very notion of racial authenticity, of Blackism, Schuyler dismissed as a rationalist fiction. A multiracial universe promises to be as devoid of "self-made" races as the real world of numerous communities—"little platoons," as Burke referred to those institutions intermediate between governments and their citizens—promises to be devoid of "self-made" individuals. In "Negro-Art Hokum," Schuyler remarks: "Negro art there has been, is, and will be among the numerous black nations of Africa; but to suggest the possibility of any such development among the ten million colored people in this republic is self-evident foolishness." [388]

It is true that blacks gave rise to "those slave songs based on Protestant hymns and Biblical texts known as the spirituals, works songs and secular songs of sorrow and tough luck known as the blues," as well as "jazz" and "the Charleston," but there is nothing distinctively, much less uniquely, *black* or "Negro" about any of this. Rather, these are the "contributions of a caste" dwelling "in a certain section of the country"—namely, the Southeast. These same art forms are "foreign to Northern Negroes, West Indian Negroes, and African Negroes." Thus, they no more reflect what today is often called "the black experience in America" than does "the music and dancing of the Appalachian highlanders or the Dalmatian peasantry" reflect "the Caucasian race."

Other genres of so-called "Negro art" are even more obviously Eurocentric. The "literature, painting, and sculpture" of black Americans "is identical in kind with the literature, painting, and sculpture of white Americans: that is, it shows more or less evidence of European influence." Schuyler offers the examples of "the dean of Aframerican literati," W.E.B. Du Bois, "the foremost Aframerican sculptor," Meta Warwick Fuller, and Henry Ossawa Tanner, "the most noted Aframerican painter...." Du Bois was educated at Harvard and at universities in Germany, Fuller is a one-time pupil of Rodin, and Tanner, being the "dean of painters in Paris," was at one time "decorated by the French Government." It is folly of the first order to hold up the work of these artists as embodying something uniquely, or even distinctively, black.

That so-called "Negro art" is nothing of the kind is what we should expect once we consider that "the Aframerican is merely a lampblacked Anglo-Saxon." [389] How could he not be? After all, "the Aframerican is subject to the same economic and social forces that mold the actions and thoughts of the white Americans." [390] Given that blacks have been in America "for the last three hundred years," [391] and given that black and white Americans of comparable cultural and economic circumstances have "similar furniture, literature, and conversation," it should come as no surprise that the arts produced by blacks should "reveal the psychology and culture of their environment"—*not* "their color." [392]

In addition to his historical and tradition-centered views on race relations and racial identity, Schuyler's opposition to the rationalism of the Blackist found expression as well in his orientation toward liberty—an orientation that in turn reflected his conception of change.

In 1963, when the historic Civil Rights Act of the following year was still just a bill, Schuyler came out forcefully against it. Though each of the multiple lines of attack that he launched is distinct from the others, they all speak to the various ways in which the bill reflects and advances an unmistakably rationalist—i.e. utopian—agenda. Its architects are typical rationalists inasmuch as they presumably believe both that legislation is *necessary* if constructive social change is to be had and that legislation is the *sole* way to affect *rapid* social change. However, on both counts, they couldn't be more mistaken.

The propensity "to speed social change by law," a predilection that distinguishes all relatively young countries like the United States that suffer from "a passion for novelty," the offspring of the union of "moral indignation" and the desire for "social reform," is rooted in the bogus "assumption that by such legerdemain it is possible to make people better by *force.*" Yet although this strikes its advocates as both possible and desirable, this piece of self-delusion "has been the cause of much misery and injustice throughout the ages." [393] In reality, "it is almost axiomatic that it takes lots of time to change social mores, especially with regard to such hardy perennials as religion, race and nationality, to say nothing of social classes." [394]

Schuyler acknowledges that (as of 1963) changes in race relations have been "very slow;" but he is also quick to point out that they have been "marked"—particularly during the last 25 years or so preceding the composition of his argument.

Furthermore, these changes are of such quality that no other country on Earth can claim to have given rise to anything remotely comparable to them as far as dealings with their own racial minorities are concerned. In terms of "education, housing, health, voting and economic well-being," black Americans by far and away eclipse the material condition of the racial minorities of other societies, including and especially those societies—like India, Soviet Russia, Japan, Indonesia, Australia, and countries throughout Latin America—"whose spokesmen criticize and excoriate the United States...." Schuyler draws our attention to the fact that civil rights laws, whether "state or federal, have had little to do with" any of this progress in America. Moreover, such laws "have been enforced and accepted only when the dominant majority acquiesced;" otherwise, they "have generally lain dormant in the law books."

In other words, it is not legislation that inspires human conduct; rather, it is "custom" that "has dictated the pace of compliance" with legislation.

There is one other critical respect—perhaps, from Schuyler's perspective, *the most* critical respect—in which the proposed civil rights legislation betrays its debt to rationalism. What would become the Civil Rights Act of 1964 relies upon an abstract notion of liberty. Schuyler knew that the liberty to which Americans of all backgrounds have grown accustomed—the liberty with which they were, or at least claimed to be, in love—is not some abstract, timeless universal principle or ideal but a concrete, culturally-specific complex of institutional arrangements guaranteeing a vast diffusion of power and authority. It was precisely because federal civil rights laws of the sort being proposed threatened to upset this arrangement that he invoked this as "the principal" consideration against it.

A federal civil rights law "is...another encroachment by the central government on the federalized structure of our society." Such a law, though intended to "improve the lot of a tenth of the population," will render it that much easier for the government to "enslave the rest of the populace," for under it, "the individual everywhere" will be "told what he must do and what he cannot do, regardless of the laws and ordinances of his state or community." But "this is a blow at the very basis of American society," a society "founded on state sovereignty and individual liberty and preference." Schuyler writes: "We are fifty separate countries…joined together for mutual advantage, security, advancement, and protection. It was never intended that we should be bossed by a monarch, elected or born." Schuyler concludes: "When this happens, the United States as a free land will cease to exist." [395]

Conclusion

Schuyler's critics' judgments to the contrary notwithstanding, Schuyler did not, as Jeffrey Leak remarks, abandon "racial justice" in favor of "extreme forms of conservative ideology;" [396] much less was he a "race traitor." [397] As I have argued here, Schuyler's critics, like Jeffrey Leak, have grossly oversimplified Schuyler in viewing him as an ultimately insensitive—and insensible—ideologue when it came to race relations in America. Rather, Schuyler was an adherent of a classical conservative intellectual tradition that was born of resistance to the rationalistic excesses of Enlightenment. His epistemic, ethical, and political conceptions—specifically, his tradition-centered philosophies of race, identity, and liberty—were molded within the context of this centuries-old contest, for it was against the latest manifestation of rationalism—Blackism—that Schuyler found himself laboring mightily.

Chapter 7

CONSERVATISM AND "RACISM": DECONSTRUCTING AN UNWIELDY CONCEPT

Introduction

IN ST. JOHN'S Gospel, the evangelist writes that such was the bulk of Jesus' deeds that all of the books in the world couldn't contain accounts of them.[398] The same could be said about the number of definitions of "racism" with which contemporary Westerners must reckon. "Racism" is used in a bewildering variety of contexts, applied alike to thoughts, words, and deeds; to individual persons, communities, and even social institutions. The most benevolent of human beings no less than the most ruthless of ethnic cleansers have been accused of "racism."

Still, despite—or, perhaps, because of—the relentless frequency with which charges of "racism" are hurled about, there is nothing even remotely approximating a consensus on what "racism" *is*. To judge from the tireless preoccupation of the *Zeitgeist's* movers and shakers—academics, artists, media personalities, and politicians—we can only infer that "racism" is ubiquitous, even if not necessarily overt. In addition to this, everyone seems to agree that "racism" is not only evil, but maybe even *uniquely* evil: the very *accusation* of "racism" is enough to guarantee a humiliating social death for the accused. Indeed, not infrequently, even convicted murderers aren't stigmatized as harshly as are accused "racists." [399]

Yet at least we know what murder is. In contrast, it is precisely because of the indiscriminateness with which we apply the term "racism" that suspicions arise that we don't know what "racism" is just because *there's nothing there to know*: if *every*one and every*thing* is "racist," then *no one* and *nothing* is "racist."

In this paper, I divest "racism" of its standard role of plaintiff and assign to it that of defendant. My objective is to substantiate two theses.

First, in spite of what the singularity of the term "racism" suggests, there are actually *four* logically distinct conceptions or models of "racism":

1. Racism as *Racial Hatred* (RH);
2. Racism as *Racial Discrimination* (RD);
3. Racism as Doctrine of *Innate Inferiority* (II); and
4. Racism as *Institutional Racism* (IR).

Secondly, each of these models of "racism" fails to accommodate the popular, but vague, notion that "racism" is something at once ubiquitous and particularly (maybe uniquely) evil.

Exposition on "Racism" as "Racial Hatred"

Black authors Stan Faryna, Joseph G. Conti, and Brad Stetson endorse "racial humanism," a vision of race and humanity that they attribute to Martin Luther King, Jr. "Racial humanism" is deliberately intended as an antidote to the view that "racism" is a uniquely white phenomenon, what Conti and Stetson call "institutional" or "structural racism." The view that "only whites can be racist" is a species of "collectivist and deterministic thinking" that stands "in stark contrast" to the view, central to "racial humanism," "that anyone who hates on the basis of race is a racist."

Take the instances of Reginald Denny, "the [white] truck driver beaten nearly to death during the 1992 Los Angeles riots [by black rioters]," and Colin Ferguson, the black gunman who murdered several whites and Asians on a New York commuter train. Conti and Stetson insist that Denny and the families of Ferguson's victims "know full well that African Americans—like all human beings—can be racists." [400]

Racism is an "evil," but it is "an individual shortcoming" to which "everyone—whatever their ethnicity or class" is susceptible," [401] for anyone can *hate* "on the basis of race." [402]

Critique

At first glance, the RH model of "racism" is both simple and uncontroversial. Yet appearances can be deceptive. RH is not without its problems.

First, if racial hatred is immoral, then is this because *hatred*, irrespective of its object, is immoral? If so, then this claim is in desperate need of an argument, for the proposition that hatred is *always* immoral is most definitely *not* axiomatic. Still, even if it *was* self-evident, or even if a compelling argument for its truth was in the coming, RH would still have its work cut out for it. The problem is that if racial hatred is immoral because *hatred* is immoral, then, morally, *the object* of hatred is irrelevant. *Racial* hatred is neither more nor less noxious than hatred of serial murderers, rapists, Christians, and the left-handed. That it is the members of other races that happen to be hated is morally inconsequential.

But suppose RH claims not that racial hatred is wrong because hatred is always wrong, but that racial hatred is wrong because race is a *morally irrelevant* consideration and it is always wrong to hate on the basis of *morally irrelevant* considerations. Racial hatred is wrong, then, for the same reason that hatred of acne-inflicted people is wrong. To this line, three replies are in order.

For starters, when it is claimed that some feature or other (like race) is of no moral relevance, it is far from clear what this is supposed to mean. The implication seems to be that there is a sort of one-size-fits-all index of moral relevance, and by this measure, race *always* lacks moral relevance. This, however, is not only questionable; given that race is among a constellation of contingencies that shape and reflect both personal identity and culture, it seems likely that, to no slight extent, what's morally relevant is determined by the particularities of one's historical-cultural context.

Yet even on the assumption that there *is* a universal or absolute criterion of moral relevance, there remains a prima facie case for *rejecting* the notion that race is not morally relevant. Consider: if race is as morally irrelevant as is a pimple, then it is just as irrational for human beings to regard their race as a defining feature of their identity as it is irrational to regard a pimple as a defining feature of identity. But people *do* view race as at least *a* defining aspect of their identity. Racial talk, unlike talk of acne, isn't just morally charged (though it is this); it is (far too often) morally *explosive*.

Of course, the point here isn't that race *is* morally relevant. The point is that proponents of RH (and anyone else, for that matter) have no warrant for *assuming* that it's *not*. If the claim is that while we do treat race *as if* it is morally relevant, we are mistaken in doing so—it is "*racist*" to do so—then it should be clear that this is a viciously question-begging definition of "racism," for whether we are mistaken in regarding race as possessing moral relevance is the point that's in dispute.

There is, though, a third problem with RH, a problem that arises from the assumption that race is morally neutral. If it is the *moral irrelevance* of race that makes race-based hatred immoral, then the fact that *race* happens to be the morally irrelevant characteristic in question is neither here nor there.

"Racism" is relegated to the moral periphery, being no better or worse than hatred based upon any other morally irrelevant feature or set of features.

There remain still other difficulties with identifying "racism" with racial hatred. Whether proponents of RH claim that it is always wrong to hate or always wrong to hate on the basis of morally irrelevant features, they must come to terms with the fact that hatred is an ambiguous concept. Considered as a condition of the heart, it's something that only God can know. Human beings must judge on the basis of actions, actions that both reveal and form character. Yet hatred, like any other sentiment, is intrinsically indeterminate vis-à-vis actions. As Michael Oakeshott states, "an agent's choice or disposition to respond to his situation in, for example, a motive of charitableness, of fear, or of avarice [or of hatred] is not itself the choice of a response," for a person "may kill in a sentiment of compassion or of hatred; he may mean to keep a promise in a motive of greed, of gratitude, or of resentment; he may concern himself with another's wants out of fear, kindness, pity, or contempt." [403] Hatred doesn't necessarily lead to cruelty of the sort of which Reginald Denny's attackers and Colin Ferguson were guilty, or cruelty of any sort at all, and cruelty can follow just as readily from indifference and even love as it can follow from hatred.

What this implies is that, by the lights of RH, a person who hates, a "racist," *need not* act cruelly, while a person who acts cruelly but who doesn't hate is not a "racist."

The RH model of "racism," I conclude, is inadequate. Its dependence upon questionable assumptions fails to distinguish "racism" as the ubiquitous, especially awful phenomenon that contemporary convention would have us believe that it is. In fact, it fails to distinguish "racism" as any kind of phenomenon at all.

Exposition on "Racism" as "Racial Discrimination"

"Racism" is also widely equated with "racial discrimination." For example, in his attempt to refute "ethical egoism"—the theory that morality requires that agents always act so as to advance their own self-interests—James Rachels compares it to "racism." Both "moral doctrines" consist in "dividing people into groups," and both refuse to treat "the interests" of these groups equally. "Racism," Rachels asserts, like "anti-Semitism," "nationalism," and, of course, "ethical egoism," has "the practical result…that members of the preferred" group "are to be treated better than the others." [404]

Rachels says that such views are indefensible, for they are incapable of surmounting the "general principle" that we're justified in "treating people differently only if we can show that there is some factual difference between them that is relevant to justifying the difference in treatment." [405]

To bring this principle into focus, Rachels invokes the example of a law school admissions' procedure.

The decision to select one applicant over another for admission into law school is "justified" as long as it can be shown that, say, the person selected "graduated from college with honors and scored well on the admissions test, while" the person rejected "dropped out of college and never took the test."

Suppose, though, that both applicants are comparably qualified but there is a place for only one of them. In such a situation, the decision to choose one over the other will be "arbitrary" and, thus, immoral.

Because there are no morally relevant differences between persons that could rationally justify its demand that individuals ascribe greater weight to their own interests than that which they attach to the interests of others, "ethical egoism," according to Rachels, is "unacceptably arbitrary."

Similarly, "racism" is "unacceptably arbitrary" [406] insofar as it requires, in the absence of morally relevant distinctions between races, intra-racial partiality.

Critique

Before proceeding, it should be noted that the RD conception of "racism" is logically independent of the RH model. According to the latter, as we have seen, hatred of the members of other races is both necessary and sufficient for "racism." But, according to the RD model, hatred is neither necessary nor sufficient: hatred *can* lead to racial discrimination, it is true, but so too can any other sentiment, including the sentiment of *love*. In fact, love for, or at least partiality *toward*, the members of one's *own* race has not infrequently accounted for "racial discrimination."

But RD has its own share of problems. If partiality toward one's own interests and the interests of the members of one's race is immoral because it is "unacceptably arbitrary," then why isn't partiality toward the interests of one's spouse or children over the interests of the spouses and children of others not "unacceptably arbitrary?" If there are no "factual differences" that could possibly justify preferential treatment in the former cases, then it is hard to conceive of "factual differences" that could justify preferential treatment in the latter cases. However, scarcely anyone thinks that a man has the same obligations to another man's wife and children as he has to his own. But if he doesn't act wrongly in showing partiality toward his own family, then how can it be that he acts wrongly in showing partiality toward his own self, his nation, and his race? Conversely, if morality *precludes* partiality toward oneself, one's nation, and one's race, then why does it not preclude partiality toward one's family?

Secondly, proponents of RD need to specify if racial discrimination amounts to "racism" when race is used as *the sole* or just *the primary* criterion in making judgments. Either way, as Rachels makes clear, racial discrimination is evil because race is a morally irrelevant characteristic. However, as was noted above, what counts as "morally irrelevant" cannot be determined in advance of circumstances. Race *may* be morally *relevant,* depending on context. Hence, inasmuch as RD rules this possibility out from the outset and equates racial discrimination with "racism," it supplies us with an account of "racism" that is no less question-begging than the RH model.

Moreover, whether it is the use of race as the sole or primary criterion that is objectionable, what's objectionable is the employment of *any* (allegedly) morally irrelevant characteristic in a decision-making procedure. If this, though, is the case, then racial discrimination *per se* is neither distinctively nor, much less, uniquely evil. That the morally irrelevant characteristic in question *happens* to be race is beside the point.

Yet suppose that the claim here is that "racism" occurs when race is employed as the sole criterion in judgment-making. If this is so, then not only is "racism" not ubiquitous; it is quite possibly *nonexistent,* for in our daily interactions, neither race nor any other criterion functions independently of other contextual considerations. Race is an abstraction, but even our theoretical understandings of it are invariably accompanied by a complex of notions—cultural patterns, biological traits, etc.—that are conceptually distinct from "color." When it comes to the concrete decision-making of everyday life, race is all the more tethered to a plethora of other characteristics like age, gender, dress attire, patterns of speech, and so forth. In short, race encompasses more than *color.* To put it starkly, no one ever perceives *just* color.

If defenders of RD mean to say that it is immoral, "racist," to use race as the *primary* criterion in decision-making, the burden is on them, then, to explain why it is permissible to use race as *a* criterion at all, for if what makes the use of race evil is that it is morally irrelevant, then the use of race is immoral whether it functions primarily *or minimally* in decision making. But there exists a variety of unobjectionable social practices in which race *is,* at the very least, *a* factor. For example, no one criticizes, say, a Chinese restaurant owner for hiring his co-ethnics in order to lend an air of "authenticity" to his enterprise. Neither has there ever been any handwringing over the FBI's time-honored practice of employing race as an index in profiling serial killers. Similarly, there is little outcry over the fact that, irrespective of race, the vast majority of human beings *living in interracial societies* routinely permit racial considerations to inform their practices of dating, marrying, adoption, etc.

There is, though, one *controversial* practice in which race figures predominantly but to which, interestingly, no small supply of *defenders* of the RD model—like James Rachels, for instance—have actually lent support: "affirmative action." The latter is a primarily race-based preferential treatment policy that renders it illegal for employers and college admissions offices to *not* discriminate *in favor* of blacks and other non-whites over whites (and sometimes Asians).

Now, if it is morally legitimate to not only allow for racial discrimination but to *coerce* select groups to engage in racial discrimination for the purposes of ostensibly benefitting people of color—if, in other words, it is a moral imperative to use race as a primary criterion in discriminating against whites—then either the proponents of RD have just contradicted their own account of "racism" *or,* what is just as problematic, they have introduced an as-of-yet unheard of distinction between "racism" that is bad and "racism" that is *good*: "racism" is bad when race is used to discriminate against people of color but good when used to discriminate in favor of people of color—or against whites.

In conclusion, the RD model of "racism" must be rejected. Not only is it question-begging, but however it is read, it fails to show either that "racism" is ubiquitous or that it is uniquely evil. Moreover, RD implies that "racism" may even be a moral requirement!

Exposition on "Racism" as Doctrine of "Innate Inferiority" (II)

An older definition of "racism," and one that persists to the present, is offered by Dinesh D'Souza in *The End of Racism*. The author concedes that the plurality of contexts within which it has been used has rendered the term "racism" a complicated one, yet he nevertheless holds that, at its core, "racism" means now what it has meant for the last two centuries. It denotes "an ideology of intellectual or moral superiority based upon the biological characteristics of race," and it "typically entails a willingness to discriminate based upon a perceived hierarchy of superior and inferior races." [407] So, a "racist" is one who believes in the innate inferiority of the members of races other than his own and *may* discriminate against them on that basis.

Critique

The first observation to make here is that II presupposes neither hatred nor, *necessarily*, racially discriminatory conduct on the part of its proponents. It is neither a sentiment, like hatred, nor an action, like discrimination. It is, principally, an idea or belief.

The first problem, however, in identifying an (allegedly) evil, perhaps a *uniquely* evil, phenomenon like "racism" with a belief is that beliefs, embodying as they do judgments regarding reality, may be *true* or *false*—not moral or immoral. It's impossible to imagine circumstances under which a true belief could be immoral. Yet it's also not easy to envision how a false belief could be thought to be immoral on account of its falsity. Was Ptolemy immoral for believing that the sun revolved around the Earth? Is a loving wife immoral for having believed that her adulterous husband was faithful to her?

There's no sense to be gotten from speaking of a true belief as immoral, but neither is it much more sensible to speak of a false belief as being immoral just because of its falsity. Yet it is *not* the falsity of a belief per se that renders it immoral, objectors will insist. What convicts a false belief of immorality is the evil purpose or purposes in the service of which it has been or can be enlisted. This objection, however, proves both too much and too little.

On the one hand, II need not be appropriated for the sake of serving any wicked goals and, in fact, it may even inspire *benevolent* action on the part of those who subscribe to it. At any rate, belief in the innate inferiority of other races in no way precludes benevolent treatment of their members. For that matter, belief in II in no way precludes belief in *the inherent equality* of *all* human beings in the eyes of God, say, or insofar as "natural rights" or "human rights" are concerned. Take Thomas Jefferson, for instance. Though a slave master, Jefferson was also a vehement opponent of slavery. While admitting to entertaining "doubts" regarding "the grade of understanding allotted to" blacks "by nature," he was quick to point out that "whatever their degree of talent it is no measure of their rights." As he said: "Because Sir Isaac Newton was superior to others in understanding, he was not therefore lord of the person or property of others." [408]

Belief in the innate intellectual and/or moral inferiority of others human beings, whether they be the members of one's own race or those of another, is compatible, both in thought and in practice, with a belief in their equal worth or dignity and a commitment to their equal treatment. As D'Souza says, II has been held "by many of *the most enlightened, courageous*, and *humane* figures in America and the West," figures like David Hume, Immanuel Kant, and Georg Hegel. [409]

This should be unsurprising, for belief in the innate inferiority of *animals,* and even *plants*—i.e. "the environment"—need not, and often is not, accompanied by cruelty toward these non-human life forms. Sometimes, as is the case with many Jews and Christians who view themselves as divinely appointed stewards of God's creation, it is precisely the belief in the human being's innate *superiority* over all other living things that results in the former making tremendous efforts to extend care and benevolence toward the latter.

On the other hand, subscription to II proves too much, for if its reasoning is taken to its extreme logical term, we'd have to conclude that it can be immoral to hold even beliefs that many of us assume are *true*. After all, as a matter of historical fact, there is no question that beliefs in liberty, equality, virtue, piety, and justice *have* led to evil. So, if it is the evil actions that are performed, or that could be performed, on the basis of a belief that make that belief, or the holding of that belief, evil, then both false and true beliefs are evil, for evil has been done in the name of ideas that are both false and true. This, of course, also implies the absurd conclusion that, since the proponents of every moral ideal have done evil for its sake, subscription to morally righteous (and presumably true) beliefs is just as evil as subscription to morally rotten (and false) beliefs. Thus, belief in II is no more and no less immoral than any and every other belief!

A final consideration to bear in mind is the sheer fact that, if "racism" is simply belief in II, then not only is there no sense in which it can be declared especially evil, or even evil at all; it must be very rare to boot, for few if any people any longer endorse it.

The II model of "racism," we must conclude, fares no better than the RH and RD models in accommodating the popular, but, thus far, groundless notion, that "racism" is something at once ubiquitous and especially evil.

Exposition on "Racism" as "Institutional Racism"

"Institutional racism" involves no individual hatred, discrimination, or belief in innate inferiority on the part of whites. Richard Wasserstrom writes that "institutional racism" is both "unintentional" and "more subtle" than both "overt or covert racial discrimination by state action, which is now banished, and racial prejudice, which still lingers, but only in the hearts of persons...." It consists of "institutions and practices [that] very often, if not always, reflect in important and serious ways a variety of dominant values in the operation of what is apparently a neutral legal mechanism," as well as latent ideas on which we regularly depend that, when taken in conjunction with each other, guarantee "the maintenance and reinforcement of a system in which whites dominate over non-whites."[410]

Iris Marion Young goes further in claiming that the ideal of "assimilation," presupposing, as it does, the ideal of a "color-blind" society, serves to reinforce long-standing patterns of oppression. Even though "the ideal of a common humanity in which all can participate without regard to race, gender, religion, or sexuality poses as neutral and universal," it "allows privileged groups to ignore their own group specificity" and facilitates the "disadvantage" at which "oppressed groups" find themselves.[411] The ideals of "formal equality" and "assimilation" obscure group differences that need to be made explicit if "the dominant culture" is to recognize itself "for the first time as specific: as Anglo, European, Christian, masculine, straight," and patterns that "structure privilege and oppression" are to cease.[412]

In short, "institutional racism" is the most invidious form of "racism," for insofar as it is constitutive of the fundamental institutions and assumptions of American life, procedures and laws that appear to be race-neutral but which in reality embody "Eurocentric" and "masculine" prejudices that "privilege" white males while perpetuating the oppression of all other groups, it is like the air we breathe: ubiquitous and thus, invisible.

Critique

The IR model of "racism" excludes all considerations concerning the particularities of flesh and blood persons. It is as abstract a theory of "racism" available to us. And, it is *deliberately* so. The abstractness of IR serves as a virtue by investing it with an air of plausibility that it otherwise wouldn't possess. Its strength, however, is also its vice, for by neglecting the concrete relativities and contingencies of the individual human interactions of everyday life, IR seeks to immunize itself against refutation. Nevertheless, the inadequacies of IR can be disclosed easily enough.

Before proceeding further, the viciously circular reasoning of IR must first be made explicit. Its proponents note gross statistical disparities between blacks as a group and whites as a group. From this fact, they infer a cause: "racism." But the only way the proponents of IR can get to this conclusion is by way of the premise that "racism," and *only* "racism," can cause statistical disparities of the sort that exist between blacks and whites. The problem here, though, is that the proponents of IR *cannot* rely upon this premise without begging the question, for this premise is nothing other than *the conclusion* that they need to prove.

And the assumption that only "racism" could give rise to interracial statistical inequalities does indeed need argument, for not only is it not axiomatic, it is dubious.

Black American scholar Thomas Sowell has been a student of racial and ethnic differences for decades. He informs us that "international studies have repeatedly shown gross intergroup disparities to be commonplace all over the world, whether in alcohol consumption, fertility rates, educational performance, or innumerable other variables." Sowell remarks that "a reasonably comprehensive listing of such disparities would be at least as large as a dictionary" [413]—and there is nothing nefarious about any of them. American men, for instance, are struck by lightning six times as often as are American women, and during the 1960's in Malaysia, degrees in higher education were overwhelmingly concentrated in the hands of the Chinese minority. To underscore just how "absurd" is the claim that statistical disparities between groups, whether racial or otherwise, must be the function of a wicked phenomenon (like "racism"), Sowell observes that as far back as 1985, twice as many Asian Americans as whites scored over 700 on the mathematical section of the Scholastic Aptitude Test.[414] Moreover, he notes that there is a "gross disparity in 'representation' between blacks and whites in professional basketball," and a "gross 'overrepresentation' of blacks among the highest-paid players in baseball"—and yet neither of these patterns is considered proof of "discrimination" against whites.

Consistency, however, demands that the defenders of IR view it as such, for the very same "procedure" that leads to these results "is being taken in deadly seriousness" when it is blacks who are at a disadvantage relative to whites. When the latter obtains, "racism" becomes the only factor that explains the "under representation" of blacks in various facets of life.[415]

Thirdly, IR relies upon data concerning monolithic abstractions, racial categories that swallow up the many *intra-racial* differences that bring into focus a picture of race relations in America that is not only profoundly different from that painted by IR; the former picture *undercuts* the latter.

When relevantly similar subsets of blacks and whites are compared we discover that whatever disparities existed between "blacks" and "whites" either diminish dramatically or vanish altogether. For example, as far back as 1969, and two years *before* "affirmative action," Sowell notes that "blacks and whites whose homes included newspapers, magazines, and library cards, and who had also gone on to obtain the same number of years of schooling" had the same average income. Beginning in the early 1970's, "young black husband-wife families outside the South have had incomes virtually identical to those of young white husband-wife families outside of the South," and in some years have actually earned a bit more than their white counterparts.[416] As of the early to mid-1980's, "where husbands and wives are both college-educated, and both working, black families of this description earn slightly *more* than white families of this description--nationwide and without regard to age." [417]

A final consideration against IR is that it is modally confused: *persons* or *individuals* are moral or immoral, "racist" or not; *institutions*, however, are efficient or inefficient, productive or unproductive. Whatever other definitions or conceptions of "institution" may be available, it is certain that proponents of IR view an "institution" as an impersonal or trans-personal entity that, as such, transcends the intentions of the persons who compose it. Hence, "institutional racism" is nothing but a synonym for, as one champion of the IR model memorably put it, "racism without racists." [418] It is no more sensible to speak of "racist" institutions than it is sensible to speak of "racist" knives or "just" houses, "tasty" planets or "bumpy" sounds.

Since IR's defenders know that it is impossible to sustain the popular thought that "racism" is both ubiquitous and especially or uniquely evil as long as "racism" is equated with racial hatred, the racially discriminatory conduct of individuals, and/or a belief in the doctrine of innate inferiority, they assume that by identifying "racism" as an attribute of *institutions* they could meet this challenge. The assumption, though, is ill-conceived: IR could establish that "racism" is a *ubiquitous* phenomenon only at the cost of *denying* that it is a *moral* one.

The theory of "institutional racism," like the other accounts of "racism" at which we have looked, fails to account for the popular idea that "racism" is pervasive and particularly evil.

Some Objections and Counter-Objections

To judge from the frequency with which the topic of "racism" recurs in our daily lives—a frequency that would lead a visitor from another planet to conclude that there is *no* topic of greater importance—it is clear that we treat as axiomatic not only the existence of "racism," but its character as a phenomenon that is at once pervasive and especially, even uniquely, evil. Considering that I have challenged this assumption, some further comments are in order.

First, to reiterate, my point here is not to deny the intelligibility of talking about "racism." What I deny is the intelligibility of how we usually *do in fact* talk about it. "Racism" may very well signify some aspect or other of human experience. But *what* exactly that experience is remains to be seen. As I've been at pains to show, as things stand, "racism" has been used in such a staggering variety of contexts that the term's been largely divested of all usefulness—and, hence, all meaning.

Secondly, even if we opt for one of the aforementioned conceptions of "racism," the latter simply cannot sustain the meaning of "racism" as something pervasive and uniquely evil that conventional usage affixes to the term.

Thirdly, that there is on the part of some individuals racial animus—animosity in which racial considerations play at least a not insignificant role—is indisputable. Yet this hardly warrants transforming this one disposition—a disposition that exists amidst a bundle of others and that can manifest itself in a virtually limitless spectrum of ways—or not manifest itself at all—into some *doctrine,* a hegemonic "ism," as it were, of epic awfulness. If racial animus is an ingredient in our understanding of an event, why not just make a note of *that*? Why go on about some devilish being we insist upon calling "racism," particularly when doing so, as I've argued, only promises to frustrate our pursuit of the very thing—understanding—for which we search? Of course, even if we *do* drop "racism" in favor of, say, "racial animus," we should remember that the latter is essentially a conceptual or epistemological tool, a descriptive, not a normative, term: its advantage over "racism" lay in its greater precision.

None of this is intended to suggest that racial animus isn't bad, much less that it is devoid of moral import. Yet if we insist on associating with "racial animus" the same connotations that we associated with "racism," we will merely replicate the difficulties with the latter that I identified in this essay: What counts as racial *animus,* and what counts as *racial* animus? Is it always wrong to experience race-based animosity and, if so, why so? And so on.

Finally, there are, sadly, some who would seek to stop this line of inquiry dead in its tracks by charging those who pursue it with—what else?—"racism." Besides being viciously question-begging—it is precisely the meaning of "racism" that's under discussion—the indictment would serve only to exacerbate further the confusion engulfing the term while vindicating the twofold suspicion that the charge of "racism" is vapid and that because of its vapidity, it is, by design, a grand conversation-stopper.

Conclusion

The commonplace assumption that "racism" is a phenomenon as ubiquitous as it is terrible both arises from and is reinforced by opinion-shapers from various precincts of our culture, from academia to politics to the media. I have argued here that this assumption has no connection with reality. While the singularity of the term "racism" implies a unitary referent, the truth of the matter is that there are four logically distinct, independent conceptions of "racism"—"Racial Hatred" (RH); "Racial Discrimination" (RD); "Innate Inferiority" (II); and "Institutional Racism" (IR). Yet none of these models is capable of sustaining the popular conception of "racism."

Chapter 8

CONSERVATISM AND HIGHER EDUCATION: LIBERAL LEARNING AS A *CONVERSATION*

Introduction

UNDOUBTEDLY, MORE CONFUSION abounds at present over the nature of a liberal arts education than can be found at any other time. In what follows, I explore three ideals—Traditionalism, Careerism, and Activism. Upon exposing their weaknesses, I take my cue from the philosopher Michael Oakeshott and advocate on behalf of imagining a liberal arts education in terms of a *conversation*. According to the latter—what, for lack of a better term, I will call "Conversationalism"—a liberal arts education hasn't any purpose *beyond itself*. In expositing upon this image of higher learning, I will contrast the nature of a conversation with two other modes of discourse with which it is commonly confused: *argument* and *inquiry*.

Traditionalism

Unlike the ideals of Careerism and Activism), the ideal of Traditionalism insists that a liberal arts education is resolutely *non*-utilitarian. From this perspective, one's decision to enter college is nothing more or less than the decision to embark upon a quest for knowledge *for the sake of knowledge*—not the sake of any *practical* concerns. The knowledge that a higher education was thought to provide is what may be called "useless" knowledge. Useless knowledge is knowledge that hasn't any obvious bearing upon the affairs of everyday life.

Traditionalism is a noble and time-honored ideal. It is to be commended for endeavoring to capture the insight that a liberal arts education was never meant to be treated as a mere means to some superior end. Still, it is not without its problems.

For starters, Traditionalism's *attempt* to establish the non-utilitarian—the purpose*less*—character of a liberal arts education must be judged a failure: the concept of knowledge for knowledge's sake and that of *a pursuit* are irreconcilable. A pursuit, after all, is, necessarily, purpose*ful*. If the purpose of a liberal arts education is to promote a pursuit, namely, the pursuit of knowledge, then it *is* subservient to securing a goal, an as-of-yet unrealized state of affairs. In Oakeshott's words, a liberal arts education, not unlike any other of the countless activities of daily life, is "teleocratic." The difficulty with this, however, is that a genuinely *disinterested* engagement, as the *pursuit* of knowledge is confusedly imagined to be, *cannot* be goal-driven or telocratic at all.

Traditionalism invokes the image of an *inquiry*. An inquiry is a *fact*-gathering mission that derives its purpose from the *conclusion(s)* in which the inquiry terminates. This presents a second challenge to Traditionalism.

Facts are items of information encapsulated in *propositions*—i.e. statements that, like the contents of any written test, can be memorized and explicitly excogitated. Knowledge, on this view, is *encyclopedic* in character, and in two respects: (1) in theory, it encompasses *all* knowable facts; (2) it is capable of being confined between the covers of a book. This being so, a liberal arts education must be deemed either a failure or a fake. There are two reasons for this.

First, however much time one commits to study, one can never hope to come even remotely close to reaching the end of the inquiry that is a liberal arts education. To put it another way, an entire universe of facts promises to remain perpetually beyond the grasp of even the most eager and devoted of students—and the most eager and devoted of *teachers*. Secondly, many, and probably most, facts that are relayed during a student's time at college are destined to be forgotten. Thus, like happiness or love, the goal of a higher education—the fulfillment of the inquiry—is sure to become that much more *elusive* the more relentlessly one pursues it.

For a suitable ideal of liberal learning we must turn elsewhere.

Careerism

From the perspective of this ideal, colleges and universities exist for the sake of securing livelihoods for students. A liberal arts education is an instrument, a sheer means to a substantive state of affairs to which it is wholly subservient, the mechanism by which graduates promise to *make money* doing what they've been prepared to do.

In spite of the popularity of this ideal, it is profoundly inadequate.

For one, if a college education derives its worth from the materially satisfying condition to which it is expected to lead, then it isn't a genuine *education* at all; it is now *training:* Careerism assimilates what was once considered a college education to training in a "vocation." The problems, though, with conceiving higher learning in terms of a vocational training are manifold.

First, considered as an ideal type, the kind of knowledge conveyed via training in a trade is what Michael Oakeshott describes as "technical knowledge," knowledge that can be "formulated into rules which are, or may be, deliberately learned, remembered" and written "down…in a book [.]"Since it "is susceptible of formulation…in propositions," technical knowledge is what may be called *propositional* knowledge. Because the latter "can be learned from a book" or "a correspondence course," it has "the appearance of certainty [.]"

However, the idea that knowledge is *essentially* propositional is an *illusion*: only *some* knowledge, and not even the better part of it at that, can be codified in propositions. Much—indeed, most—knowledge is imbibed through "continuous contact with one who is perpetually practicing it." This "practical" or "traditional knowledge," as Oakeshott characterizes it, "can neither be taught nor learned, but only imparted and acquired," and students are typically unable "to say precisely what it is."

A second problem is that as long as a liberal arts education is esteemed on account of the occupation that it is supposed to secure, we have no choice but to conclude that the study of the liberal arts is an irrational engagement, an exercise in futility, for the vast majority of classes composing a liberal arts education are simply not "relevant" to the goal of securing a lucrative career—or any kind of career.

Activism

For proponents of the Activist ideal, the purpose of a liberal arts education is the promotion of political ideals and the means by which to implement them. From this perspective, students are regarded as activists-in-training, the agents of transformative change that will bring to fruition the utopian schemes of their professors. Like its counterparts, Traditionalism and Careerism, this ideal conscripts a liberal arts education into the service of realizing some future state of affairs. The partnership between the living, the dead, and the not yet born to which Edmund Burke referred while describing civilization has no place in this scheme, for the voice of that brilliant but ever evasive future silences the voices of past and present as it beckons them to birth it into being.

One difficulty with Activism is that by subordinating education to politics—by *politicizing* education—it inevitably *destroys* education: an education that's been "politicized" is an education no more. The political is a species of the practical, precisely that mode of human activity that centers in the pursuit and obtainment of needs and desires. But a liberal arts education is distinguished precisely on account of its ability to *arrest*—not *exacerbate*—the relentless torrent of wants that we are forever trying to satisfy.

Activism too reduces a liberal arts education to *training* in a technique, fluency in propositions. Only here, the technique in question is a political *ideology*. In addition to the faulty conception of knowledge upon which it relies, Activism reduces students to ideologues in training, for the Activist ideal insists upon habituating them into assuming an *adversarial* stance toward their own civilization.

The Conversational Ideal: Education as a Conversation

Common to the Traditionalist, Careerist, and Activist ideals is the supposition that a liberal arts education consists in *the pursuit* of some substantive state of affairs that is always just beyond the horizon. But a liberal arts education is not the pursuit of a comprehensive complex of "facts," a career, or the modes of thought and techniques necessary for inaugurating a political utopia. A liberal arts education isn't a pursuit of anything at all beyond *itself*. A fitting image for it is that of a *conversation*.

A conversation, we must grasp, is neither an inquiry nor an argument. The latter are defined by their respective *goals*—their *conclusions*. Conversation, in glaring contrast, has no goal beyond itself. Michel de Montaigne communicated this insight when he said of conversation that it is "the most *delightful* activity in our lives," i.e. something worth delighting in for its own sake. Stephen Miller, author of *Conversation: A History of a Declining Art,* underscores this point when he remarks that conversation "is not instrumental." He quotes Judith Martin, the author of *Miss Manners' Guide to Excruciating Correct Behavior*:

> From the direct sales pitch to a play for the goodwill of influential people, the rule is that if it is designed to advance your career, it isn't conversation.

In elaborating upon the nature of conversation, Michael Oakeshott writes that it "is *not* an enterprise designed to yield an *extrinsic* profit;" rather, it is "an unrehearsed [i.e. *spontaneous*] intellectual adventure." Partners in conversation "are not engaged in an inquiry or a debate: there is no 'truth' to be discovered, no proposition to be proved, no conclusion sought." Thus, fellow conversationalists "are not concerned to inform, to persuade, or to refute one another;" rather, they "differ without disagreeing."

Furthermore, the knowledge to be had from inquiries and arguments is *propositional*, A different kind of knowing is to gotten from conversation, a knowledge that is less susceptible of explicit articulation, an awareness of nuances made possible by immersion in the conversation itself.

There is a third difference between conversation and its counterparts. Inquiry, ideally, is a *collective* enterprise, for fellow inquirers are joint-enterprisers whose shared resources (in time, energy, etc.) are deployed in the service of fulfilling the inquiry. Argument, given the adversarial relationship that it demands of participants, promotes a sort of radical *individualism*. In contrast to these two extremes, conversation alone requires and cultivates *individuality,* for interlocutors forge their own identities by developing their voices while simultaneously enabling others—their partners in conversation—to do the same.

Finally, conversation accommodates a plurality of very

different *kinds* of voices, like, say, "practical activity," "poetry," "science," and "history." Argument and inquiry, however, allow for *one* and *only* one kind of voice. Oakeshott describes this as the voice of "science." He notes that when "science," or "argumentative discourse," is regarded as the only legitimate voice—as it is so regarded in inquiry and argument—then "all others are acknowledged merely in respect of their aptitude to imitate" it.

There are at least three advantages to conceiving of a liberal arts education in terms of a conversation.

Firstly, the image of a conversation underscores the autonomy of each of the disciplines that compose a liberal arts education. Conversation is impossible in the absence of multiple voices, and the conversation that is the study of the liberal arts is impossible in the absence of multiple disciplines. The disciplines, in other words, are *irreducibly* distinct voices. Hence, it is as impossible as it is rude—Oakeshott calls it an exercise in "barbarism"—for any voice to evaluate others by its own standards: the integrity of each voice precludes such attempts.

This point, in turn, entails another: the cornerstone virtue inculcated by an education in the liberal arts is not, as has typically been thought, "tolerance." Rather, it is *considerateness* that enjoys this distinction. Participants in a conversation, inasmuch as they must be at least as committed to *listening* to the voices of others as they are committed to articulating their own, must be considerate of their interlocutors in two respects: They are equally obliged to contribute their respective voices to the conversation *and* permit others to do the same. *Listening*, then, is as important as *speaking*.

Thirdly, students not infrequently question "the usefulness" of their course material. Conversationalists have a reply ready at hand: A liberal arts education is no more and no less "useful" than any other *intrinsically* valuable activity like, say, friendship—or *conversation*. To borrow Oakeshott's term, a liberal arts education is resolutely not "utilitarian;" it is "*dramatic*." When the eye is on the merely useful, the desire is to *exploit*. But "use*less*" engagements are occasions in which to *delight*.

Fourthly, it is a flawed ideal of a liberal arts education that leads students' to think that their studies are irrelevant or useless. For example, if the student endorses the Careerist ideal of higher education, then he or she is bound to become disenchanted in no time with his or her studies. It isn't just that many required courses are unrelated to the careers on which students set their sights. It's also that much of what students learn in college *they forget*. And the same goes for a college education conceived in terms of the Traditionalist and Activist ideals, for both are equally thought to be *training* in *propositions*. The problem here, though, is that unless these propositions are confined to memory, the training must be deemed an abysmal failure.

According to Conversationalism, knowledge primarily consists of, not propositions, but intellectual and moral habits. As William Cory said, students "are not engaged so much in acquiring knowledge as in making mental efforts under criticism [.]" While a "certain amount of knowledge" can be secured and recollected, much is forgotten. Yet the latter is no cause for regret, "for the shadow of lost knowledge at least protects" students "from many illusions."Still, Cory asserts, an education isn't so much for "knowledge as for arts and habits [.]" A liberal arts education supplies students with "the habit of attention;" "the art of expression;" "the art of assuming at a moment's notice, a new intellectual position;" "the art of entering quickly into another person's thoughts;" "the habit of submitting to censure and refutation;" "the art of indicating assent or dissent in graduated terms;" "the habit of regarding minute points of accuracy;" and "the art of working out what is possible in a given time [.]"

A liberal arts education understood as a conversation breeds "taste, discrimination," "mental courage and mental soberness." Perhaps most importantly, an education makes possible a degree of "self-knowledge" that would have otherwise remained foreclosed to students.[419]

When a liberal arts education is understood in terms of a conversation, it is not the mastery of rules, principles, facts, methods—summarily, propositions—that is relevant. Rather, the aim of an education so conceived is the cultivation of the excellences of mind and character, head and heart, virtues— "habits and arts"—that endure long after students have obtained their degrees.

Conclusion

To sum up, I have followed the lead of Michael Oakeshott in advocating on behalf of a conversational model of higher learning. In contrasting Conversationalism with three other ideals—Traditionalism, Careerism, and Activism—I argued that only Conversationalism does justice to the non-utilitarian character that has historically been imputed to a liberal arts education. I also highlighted the differences between conversation and two other modes of discourse—inquiry and argument—in the image of which higher education has not infrequently been imagined. The image of a conversation, I contended, is at once free of the deficiencies besetting the images of inquiry and argument while promoting its own distinctive set of intellectual and moral virtues.

Chapter 9

CONSERVATISM AND HIGHER EDUCATION: THE "INABILITY TO THINK" AND MORAL GOODNESS

AS I WRITE this, the administration of St. Louis University (SLU), a Catholic institution of higher learning, has capitulated to faculty and student demands that a 19th century statue of a Jesuit missionary standing over two American Indians with a crucifix in hand be removed. The student author of an editorial published in the campus newspaper expressed the sentiments of both his peers and instructors alike when he wrote that the statue reflects "a history of colonialism, imperialism, racism and of Christian and white supremacy." [420]

Given that the statue's removal and relocation to SLU's art museum managed to garner national attention, the average person is likely under the impression that it's exceptional. It is not. In at least two fundamental respects, SLU represents the academic world at large:

1. The ideology that prevails at SLU—for lack of a better term, we'll call it "Political Correctness"—is the ideology that prevails in universities and colleges throughout the land;
2. The *activist* spirit of SLU students and their

instructors, in both substance and style, is that of students and faculty in higher education generally. There is, though, a third phenomenon of which SLU is but one of an infinite number of examples: The ideology that dominates the SLU campus is *the* Zeitgeist of contemporary Western and American culture itself—and not just of academia.[421]

In what follows, I draw on the insights of the 20th century philosopher Hannah Arendt to argue on behalf of four claims.

One: Insofar as academics promote an ideology—*any* ideology—among their students, they betray their calling to provide the latter with an *education* in the *liberal* arts. In doing so, in enslaving students to an ideology rather than liberating them with an education, professors insure that their students remain handicapped by what Arendt referred to as "the inability to think."

Two: In insuring that students become at once more knowledgeable of and more *committed* to the worldview of the larger culture, academics not only guarantee that their students will remain unable to think; they all but guarantee that their dream of unleashing upon the world student-activists who will eradicate the planet's evils comes to naught. In fact, training in the status quo is likely to *lead* to worse—not a better—world. It's likely to lead to evil.

Three: Academics can be true to their vocation to educate students into the habits of head *and* heart, of intellectual and *moral* virtue, by teaching them how to think. This, in turn, requires that they teach them *civility,* the basic manners that are the prerequisites of social intercourse. Civility is the essence of conversation. We must learn how to converse with others because in so learning we can learn how to converse *with ourselves.* And it is this ability to converse with oneself that constitutes the ability to think.

Fourth: There is an inseparable connection between the ability to think and moral goodness.

Jack Kerwick

The Ideology of the Academy and the Culture

The events at SLU described above are hardly anomalous in higher education today.

At the University of California at Berkeley, students Rodrigo Kazuo and Meg Perret published an op-ed in *The Daily Californian* in which they "call" for an "occupation of syllabi[.]" The authors insist that this demand of theirs was "instigated" by their experience in "an upper-division course in classical social theory." The syllabus for this course is scandalous, for it "employed a standardized canon of theory that began with Plato and Aristotle, then jumped to modern philosophers: Hobbes, Locke, Hegel, Marx, Weber and Foucault, all of whom are white men." Not "a single woman or person of color" was included, the students complain.

The problem, as Kazuo and Perret see it, is that these white thinkers can't relate to "the lives of marginalized peoples," or "gender or racial oppression." In fact, they didn't "even engage with the enduring legacies of European colonial expansion, the enslavement of black people and the genocide of indigenous peoples in the Americas." When "race and gender" *are* mentioned in "the white male canon," they "are at best incomplete and at worst racist and sexist." Students must "dismantle" this "tyranny," Kazuo and Perret conclude, and "demand the inclusion of women, people of color and LGBTQ* [Lesbian, Gay, Bisexual, Transgendered, Queer] authors on our curricula." [422]

Not long ago, the University of New Hampshire released its "Bias-Free Language Guide" (BFLG). The latter "is meant to serve as a starting point" in rethinking "terms related to age, race, class, ethnicity, nationality, gender, ability, sexual orientation and more" for the purpose of promoting "inclusive excellence in our campus community." In short, words that are infected with "bias" are "problematic" or "outdated;" those that are alleged to be "bias-free" are "preferred."

Some of the words that the BFLG discourages are "older

people," "elders," "seniors," and "senior citizen;" "poor person" and "person from the ghetto;" "homeless;" "obese" and "overweight;" "able-bodied" and "normal;" "blind person;" "*American*;" "foreigners;" "illegal alien;" "sexual preference;" "homosexual;" alternative "lifestyle;" "mothering;" "fathering;" and "opposite sex."

The University of New Hampshire's BFLG also identifies a number of "micro-aggressions" like the "micro-assault," the "micro-insult," and the "micro-invalidation." A micro-assault is what the guide refers to as a "verbal attack." The example used is that of one person who, upon encountering another "using a mobile chair for long distance travel," questions the latter about his or her ability to walk.

This is a micro-assault.

A micro-insult is "a form of verbal or silent demeaning through insensitive comments or behavior," and a micro-invalidation consists in "degrading a person's wholeness through making false assumptions about the other's ability, causing a sense of invalidation."[423]

Once the BFLG came to the public's attention, UNH President Mark W. Huddleston spun into damage control mode and admitted to being "troubled by many of the things in the language guide [.]" He insisted both that the guide wasn't school policy and, amazingly, that "the only NHU policy on speech is that it is free and unfettered on our campus [!]"[424]

The University of New Hampshire is far from being alone when it comes to policing language. On the other side of the country, the University of California offers its program on "Diversity and Faculty development." The program identifies a host of "micro-aggressions." It provides a chart with three columns. In the far left column are "themes." In the middle column are "micro-aggression examples." In the far right column are the "messages" that these instances of micro-aggressions convey. Here are some examples:

In complimenting a person who you suspect of being foreign born on his or her English, you communicate the message: "You are not a true American."

If, upon encountering a "person of color" who happens to be good at math, you exclaim, "Wow! How did you become so good in math?" you imply that "people of color are generally not as intelligent as Whites."

It may surprise some people to discover that appeals to "color blindness," at least when they're made by a white person—or a "*W*hite person"—indicates that the person in question "does not want to or need to acknowledge race."

Statements like, "When I look at you, I don't see color;" "There is only one race, the human race;" "America is a melting pot;" and, "I don't believe in race" are offensive. Such statements amount to whites telling non-whites: "Assimilate to the dominant culture."

Those who make these appeals to a color-blind ideal are in effect guilty of "denying the significance of a person of color's racial/ethnic experience and history," of "denying the individual as a racial/cultural being." [425]

Academia is many things, but a bastion of free and unrestricted speech is not one of them.

This ideology that is tirelessly promoted on college campuses is what is commonly regarded as "Political Correctness." While its manifestation in the academic world is more robust, more explicit, than anything that can be detected in the popular culture, the fact remains that Political Correctness *is* the dominant ideology of the culture at large. This is significant, for in substituting for education training in ideology, academics actually *frustrate* their goal to ameliorate evil. And when this ideology is the ideology of the larger culture, the likelihood that they will actually promote evil is even greater, for students are now urged to acquiesce to the mentality of the mob.

In teaching ideology, any ideology, but particularly the worldview of contemporary society, academics insure that their students will be forever hobbled by the inability to think.

The Inability to Think

Upon witnessing the trials of Adolph Eichmann and other Nazi war criminal defendants, the great 20th century philosopher Hannah Arendt noted that while Eichmann's deeds were "monstrous," he was "neither monstrous nor demonic, and the only specific characteristic one could detect…was something entirely negative"—what Arendt called "a curious, but quite authentic, inability to think." The latter, we should note, is something to which everyone is susceptible.

The inability to think is the inability to think beyond whatever the conceptual categories of the moment may happen to be. Whatever the "clichés," "stock phrases," "conventional, standardized codes of expression and conduct" may be, the inability to think *is* the inability or unwillingness to transcend them, for these safeguards "have the socially recognized function of protecting us against reality, that is, against the claim on our thinking attention which all events and facts arouse by virtue of their existence." Those "inconsistencies and flagrant contradictions" that provoke more thoughtful minds the thoughtless are immunized against.[426]

The academic's sin in promoting "non-thinking"[427] consists in denying their students the right to be autonomous or capable of self-rule. Like Eichmann, the thoughtless know and are capable of only obedience. "By shielding people against the dangers of examination," Arendt remarks, "it teaches them to hold fast to whatever the prescribed rules of conduct may be at a given time in a given society." Thus, people who are unable to think "get used to never making up their minds."[428]

In stark contrast, thought is always on the move, "defrosting"[429] some ideas while it "dissolves"[430] others. As Arendt says, the activity of thinking "is equally dangerous to all creeds [.]"[431]

Thinking is impossible in the absence of *consciousness*, literally the capacity "'to know with myself.'"[432] There is a sense, then, in which a person's mental identity, his or her consciousness, is a difference-in-unity, a two-in-one. Thinking is a conversation that transpires between the person *and him or herself*, an enterprise that "actualizes" this "difference" that is "given in consciousness" and, in so doing, *strengthens,* rather than degrades, the relationship between conversational partners.[433]

Yet neither a conversation with oneself nor with others is possible in the absence of the virtue of civility.

Civility

The virtue of civility is nothing more or less than virtue of being *mannerly*. Unlike, say, the champion of "self-expression," the mannerly person is as much, if not more, concerned with listening to others as he is with articulating his own perspective. It's not that he's averse to conflict and argument; rather, because he values *civil* disagreement, the mannerly person does his part to insure that the arguments of which he partakes are always passages within a *conversation* or *dialogue,* for only within such a context do interlocutors assume the personae of "friends."

A popular misconception of manners is that they are dispensable niceties pertaining to such things as to which sides of a dinner plate the knives and forks belong. Emily Post sets the record straight: "Manners are a sensitive *awareness of the feelings of others*. If you have that awareness, you have good manners, no matter what fork you use." In another place, she puts the point even more forcefully:

> Nothing is less important than which fork you use. Etiquette [what I am here calling manners] *is the science of living. It embraces everything. It is ethics. It is honor.*

Manners constitute "personality—the outward manifestation of *one's innate character* and attitude toward life." She adds that they "can be easily learned," for they "are like primary colors" in being "rules" that one can readily "adapt…to meet changing circumstances."[434]

Words like "please," "thank you,"[435] "you're welcome,"[436] and "hello" are "basic to civilized interaction in all societies."[437]

The mannerly person is a civil person, and the civil person is a *courteous* person, "empathetic," "flexible," "willing to adjust…to the needs and feeling of others," and "forgiving [.]"[438] Manners, then, being "the proverbial glue that holds society together," constitute the glue that joins interlocutors in conversation, for conversation is nothing other than a society of at least two selves.

Thus, in reimagining the university as a conversation, we should think of it not as a "community," but as a *"civil association,"* an association whose members, as Michael Oakeshott observes, are united not by any overarching goal, cause, or purpose—there is none; rather, members of a civil association share "a common *concern"* that the rules of civility—in our case, manners—will be met by all associates. When the university is conceived as such, it will be seen as "a moral and not a purposive association."[439]

Conclusion

I have here argued that in substituting training in an ideology for the education in head and heart that constitutes a liberal arts education, faculty not only handicap students with what Hannah Arendt described as "the inability to think;" they as well increase the likelihood that their designs for changing the world for the better via their student activists backfire, for those without the ability to think are disposed to *obey*, to acquiesce in the mentality of the herd. This risk is further increased by the fact the specific ideology of choice for contemporary academics is one and the same as that which dominates the popular culture. Moreover, I contended that in order to fulfill their obligation to enrich them both intellectually and morally, academics must educate their students in the virtue of *civility,* the art of being mannerly. Learning is inherently conversational inasmuch as conscious beings with consciences necessarily converse with both themselves and each other. But conversation is impossible without the virtue of civility.

ENDNOTES

¹ Bob Grant, *Let's Be Heard*, New York, Pocket Books, 1996, p. 100.
² For representative expressions of this conventional approach, see Tobin, Jonathan S, "The GOP Doesn't Need a Purge." *Commentary,* December 2012
www.commentarymagazine.com/2012/12/04/the-gop-doesnt-need-a-purge-tea-party-william-f-buckley/html (accessed February 28, 2014); and Welch, David, "Where Have You Gone Bill Buckley?" *The New York Times,* December 2012 www.nytimes.com/2012/12/04/opinion/where-have-you-gone-bill-buckley.html (accessed February 28, 2014)
³ From Bill Bennett's, *America: The Last Best Hope*, Nashville, Thomas Nelson, 2006, to Larry Sweikhart's and Michael Allen's *A Patriot's Guide to American History*, New York: Sentinel, 2004; from Thomas Woods' *A Politically Incorrect Guide to American History*, Washington, D.C.: Regnery, 2004; to Howard Zinn's *A People's History of the United States*, New York: Harper Collins, 1980, the temptation to invoke "history" for the sake of present political purposes knows no partisan bounds. This isn't to deny, of course, that either the aforementioned authors or anyone else who is guilty of this charge of enlisting "history" in the service of advancing an ideological agenda speak *falsely*. Rather, it's just that while their utterances may very well be *true*, they are not *historically* true.
⁴ That there is some degree of arbitrariness in my selection of conservative theorists is, of course, undeniable. However, given that, the object of this study being an intellectual tradition transcending time and place, it is also unavoidable, the goal here is not to eliminate, but to limit, the arbitrariness that's permitted to creep into this analysis. Since Burke is widely regarded as "the

patron saint of modern conservatism," it seems obvious that any examination of conservative thought that excluded Burke would be woefully inadequate. My choice of Kirk and Oakeshott, two not insignificantly different sorts of conservative thinkers from both sides of the Atlantic, is intended to show two things: first, in spite of their dissimilarities, they affirm one and the same set of philosophical concepts; secondly, these concepts have characterized conservatism in the Anglo-sphere from the time of Burke.

[5] It is worth noting that to this selection of neoconservative writers endless legions of others could have been added. The most casual perusal any random issue of *National Review*, *The Weekly Standard*, or *Commentary* unfailingly expresses the neoconservative view, as do virtually every "conservative" talk radio and Fox News host.

[6] Edmund Burke, *Reflections on the Revolution in France*, in *The Portable Edmund Burke*, ed. Isaac Kramnick, New York, Penguin Books, 1999, p. 419.

[7] Ibid., p. 424

[8] Ibid., p. 431

[9] Ibid., p. 433

[10] Ibid., p. 438

[11] Ibid., p. 448

[12] Ibid., p. 447

[13] Ibid., p. 451

[14] Ibid., p. 452

[15] Ibid., p. 458

[16] Ibid., p. 428, italics original

[17] Ibid., p. 451

[18] Ibid., p. 437

[19] Ibid., p. 451

[20] Ibid., p. 440

[21] Ibid., p. 440

[22] Ibid., p. 443

[23] Michael Oakeshott, "Talking Politics," in *Rationalism in Politics and Other Essays*, Indianapolis, Liberty Fund, 1962, p. 450, emphases added.

[24] Ibid., pp. 450-451

[25] Ibid., p. 451

[26] Edmund Burke, *Reflections on the Revolution in France*, in *The Portable*

Edmund Burke, ed. Isaac Kramnick, New York, Penguin Books, 1999, p. 442.
[27] Ibid., p. 443
[28] Michael Oakeshott, "Talking Politics," in *Rationalism in Politics and Other Essays*, Indianapolis, Liberty Fund, 1962, p. 454.
[29] Ibid., p. 455
[30] Buckley, William F., "Russell Kirk, R.I.P.," *National Review Online*, October 6, 2005
[31] Kirk, Russell, *The Conservative Mind: From Burke to Elliot*, 7th ed., Washington DC, Regnery, 1985, p. xv, emphasis original.
[32] Ibid., p. xvi
[33] Ibid., p. xv
[34] Ibid., p. xvi
[35] Ibid., p. 8
[36] Ibid., p. 9
[37] Michael Oakeshott, "On Being Conservative," in *Rationalism in Politics and Other Essay*, Indianapolis, Liberty Fund, 1962, p. 409.
[38] Ibid., p. 410
[39] Edmund Burke, *Reflections on the Revolution in France*, in *The Portable Edmund Burke*, ed. Isaac Kramnick, New York, Penguin Books, 1999, p. 428.
[40] Ibid., p. 428
[41] Quoted in Kirk's *The Conservative Mind: From Burke to Elliot*, 7th ed., Washington D.C., Regnery, 1985, p. 47.
[42] Ibid., p. 45
[43] Elliot Abrams remarks: "It is also clear that one of the most unattractive things about the opposition to neoconservatism is its inability to stay away from anti-Semitism." See his "Neoconservatism, a good idea that won't go away." *The Commentator*, June 2013 http://www.thecommentator.com/article/3758/neoconservatism_a_good_idea_that_won_t_go_away (accessed March 4, 2014)
[44] Murray, Douglas. *Neoconservatism: Why We Need It*, New York, Encounter Books, 2006, p. 38.
[45] Ibid., p. 2
[46] Strauss, Leo. *Natural Right and History*, 7th ed., Chicago, University of Chicago Press, 1970, p. 6.
[47] Ibid., p. 2

[48] Ibid., pp. 13, 14
[49] Ibid., p. 312
[50] Ibid., p. 313
[51] Bloom, Alan, *The Closing of the American Mind*, New York, Simon and Schuster, 1987, p. 39.
[52] Ibid., p. 27
[53] Ibid., p. 259
[54] Irving Kristol, "The Right Stuff," in *The Neoconservative Persuasion*, New York, Basic Books, 2011, p. 184.
[55] Kristol, "The Neoconservative Persuasion," in Ibid., p. 192.
[56] Kristol, "What is a Neoconservative?" in Ibid., p. 149.
[57] Ibid., p. 150
[58] Kristol, "'Human Rights': The Hidden Agenda," in Ibid., p. 228.
[59] Ibid., p. 227
[60] Kristol, "The Right Stuff," in Ibid., p. 182.
[61] Kristol, "'Human Rights': The Hidden Agenda," in Ibid., p. 229.
[62] Kristol, "What is a Neoconservative?" in Ibid., p. 150.
[63] Kristol, "'Human Rights': The Hidden Agenda," in Ibid., p. 227.
[64] Kristol, "American Conservatism: 1945-1995," in Ibid., p. 177, emphasis added.
[65] Kristol, "The Right Stuff," in Ibid., p. 184.
[66] Kristol, "The Neoconservative Persuasion," in Ibid., p. 192.
[67] Ibid., p. 191
[68] Bennett, William J., ed. *The Spirit of America*, New York, Touchstone, 1997, p. 26.
[69] Krauthammer, Charles, "Democratic Realism," in *Things that Matter*, New York, Random House, 2013, p. 346.
[70] Ibid., p. 347
[71] Ibid., p. 355
[72] Ibid., p. 340
[73] Ibid., p. 345
[74] Ibid., p. 347
[75] Ibid., p. 348, emphasis original.
[76] Prager, Dennis, "Who Believes in American Exceptionalism? Judeo-Christian Values part XXIV," *Townhall.com,* November 2005, http://townhall.com/columnists/dennisprager/2005/11/01/who_believes_in_american_exceptionalismnbsp;_judeo-christian_values_part_xxiv (accessed March 4, 2014)

[77] http://townhall.com/columnists/michaelmedved/2011/04/05/view_of_us_shapes_libcon_divide

[78] Michael Oakeshott, "On Being Conservative," in *Rationalism in Politics* (Indianapolis: Liberty Fund, 1962).

[79] Irving Kristol, "America's 'Exceptional' Conservatism," in *Neoconservatism: The Autobiography of an Idea* (New York: The Free Press, 1995), p. 373.

[80] Ibid., p. 374.
[81] Ibid., p. 375.
[82] Ibid., p. 376.
[83] Ibid., p. 377.
[84] Ibid., p. 407.

[85] Michael Oakshott, "On Being Conservative," in *Rationalism in Politics* (Indianapolis: Liberty Fund, 1962), p. 408.

[86] Ibid., p. 414.
[87] Ibid., p. 408.
[88] Ibid., p. 410.
[89] Ibid., p. 413.
[90] Ibid., p. 409.
[91] Ibid., p. 412.
[92] Ibid., p. 417.
[93] Ibid., p. 416.
[94] Ibid., p. 417.

[95] Augustine. *The Confessions of St. Augustine*. Trans. John K. Ryan (New York: DoubleDay, 1960), p. 255.

[96] Ibid., p. 287.
[97] Ibid., p. 296.
[98] Ibid., p. 302, emphases mine.

[99] Blaise Pascal. *Pensees*. Trans. A.J. Krailsheimer (New York: Penguin Books, 1995), p. 13.

[100] Michael Oakeshott, "On Being Conservative," in *Rationalism in Politics and Other Essays*. (Indianapolis: Liberty Fund, 1962), pp. 422-423).

[101] Ibid., p. 423.
[102] Ibid., p. 424.
[103] Ibid., p. 427.
[104] Ibid., p. 411.

[105] Ibid., pp. 411-412.
[106] Irving Kristol, "America's 'Exceptional' Conservatism," in *Neoconservatism: An Autobiography of an Idea* (New York: The Free Press, 1995), p. 377.
[107] Ibid., pp. 373-374.
[108] Edmund Burke's, "Reflections on the Revolution in France", in *The Portable Edmund Burke*. Ed. Isaac Kramnick (New York: Penguin Books, 1990), p. 428.
[109] Ibid., pp. 424-425.
[110] Ibid., p. 456.
[111] Ibid., p. 457.
[112] Ibid., p. 452.
[113] Ibid., p. 444
[114] Ibid., p. 445.
[115] Ibid., p. 440.
[116] Ibid., p. 448.
[117] Ibid., p. 450.
[118] Michael Oakeshott, "Rationalism in Politics," in *Rationalism in Politics and Other Essays* (Indianapolis: Liberty Fund, 1962), p. 33 emphases mine.
[119] Ibid., p. 32.
[120] Ibid., pp. 32-33.
[121] Edmund Burke, "Speech on Conciliation with the Colonies," in *The Portable Edmund Burke*. Ed. Isaac Kramnick (New York: Penguin Books, 1990), p. 261 emphases mine.
[122] Edmund Burke, "Address to the British Colonists in North America," in *The Portable Edmund Burke*. Ed. Isaac Kramnick (New York: Penguin Books, 1990), emphases mine.
[123] Michael Oakeshott, "Rationalism in Politics," in *Rationalism in Politics and Other Essays* (Indianapolis: Liberty Fund, 1962), p. 32.
[124] Ibid., p. 41
[125] Andrew Oldenquist, "Loyalties," in *Patriotism,* ed. Igor Prmoratz (Amherst: Humanity Books, 2002), p. 25.
[126] Hayek, F.A. *The Fatal Conceit* (Chicago: The University of Chicago Press, 1988).
[127] Voegelin, Eric. *Science, Politics, and Gnosticism* (New York: Regnery, 1968).
[128] Graves, Robert. *King Jesus,* 1st ed. (New York: Farrar, Straus and

Giroux, 1981).
[129] John Locke, *An Essay Concerning Human Understanding,* ed. Kenneth Winkler (Cambridge: Hackett, 1996).
[130] Edmund Burke, "Reflections on the Revolution in France," in *The Portable Edmund Burke,* ed. Isaac Kramnick (New York: Penguin Books, 1999), p. 437.
[131] Oakeshott, Michael, "Rationalism in Politics," in *Rationalism in Politics and Other Essays* (Indianapolis: Liberty Fund, 1962), p. 40.
[132] Ibid., p. 15.
[133] Ibid., p. 16.
[134] David McCabe, "Patriotic Gore, Again," in *Patriotism,* ed. Igor Primoratz (Amherst: Humanity Books, 2002), p. 122.
[135] Paul Gomberg, "Patriotism is Like Racism," in *Patriotism,* ed. Igor Primoratz (Amherst: Humanity Books, 2002), p. 105.
[136] Ibid., p. 106.
[137] Ibid. p. 107.
[138] Alasdair MacIntyre, "Is Patriotism a Virtue?" in *Patriotism,* ed. Igor Primoratz (Amherst: Humanity Books, 2002), p. 44.
[139] Ibid., p. 45.
[140] Ibid., p. 57.
[141] Ibid., p. 44.
[142] Ibid., p. 45.
[143] Ibid., p. 47.
[144] Murray, Douglas. *Neoconservatism: Why We Need It* (New York: Encounter Books, 2006), p. 2.
[145] Strauss, Leo. *Natural Right and History.* 7th ed. (Chicago: University of Chicago Press, 1970), p. 2.
[146] Ibid., p. 5.
[147] Ibid., p. 14.
[148] Ibid., p. 13.
[149] Bloom, Allan. *The Closing of the American Mind* (New York: Simon & Schuster, 1987), p. 39.
[150] Ibid., p. 27.
[151] Ibid., p. 259.
[152] Murray, Douglas. *Neoconservatism: Why We Need It* (New York: Encounter Books, 2006), p. 59.
[153] Ibid., p. 38.
[154] Ibid., p. 73.

[155] Kristol, Irvin, "What is a Neoconservative?" in *The Neoconservative Persuasion* (New York: Basic Book, 2011), p. 150

[156] Kriston, Irvin, "'Human Rights': The Hidden Agenda," in *TNP*, p. 228.

[157] Ibid., p. 227.

[158] Kristol, Irvin, "The Right Stuff," in *TNP*, p. 182.

[159] Kristol, Irvin, "'Human Rights': The Hidden Agenda," in *TNP*, p. 229

[160] Kristol, Irvin, "What is a Neoconservative?" in *TNP*, p. 150.

[161] Kristol, Irvin, "'Human Rights': The Hidden Agenda," *TNP*, p. 227.

[162] Bennett, William J. *Why We Fight: Moral Clarity and the War on Terrorism* (New York: Double Day, 2002), p. 47.

[163] Bennett, William J., ed. *The Spirit of America* (New York: Touchstone, 1997), p. 26.

[164] Krauthammer, Charles, "Democratic Realism," in *Things that Matter* (New York: Random House, 2013), p. 346.

[165] Ibid., p. 347.

[166] Ibid., p. 345.

[167] Prager, Dennis, "Who Believes in American Exceptionalism? Judeo-Christian Values part XXIV," *Townhall.com,* November 2005 http://townhall.com/columnists/dennisprager/2005/11/01/who_believes_in_american_exceptionalismnbsp;_judeo-christian_values_part_xxiv (accessed July 24, 2015)

[168] Prager, Dennis, "Why America is Still the Best Hope," *Townhall.com* April 2012, http://townhall.com/columnists/dennisprager/2012/04/24/why_america_is_still_the_best_hope (accessed July 24, 2015)

[169] Burke, Edmund, "Reflections on the Revolution in France," in *The Portable Edmund Burke,* ed. Isaac Kramnick (New York: Penguin Books, 1999), p. 447.

[170] Ibid., p. 448.

[171] Ibid., p. 431.

[172] Ibid., p. 423.

[173] Ibid., p. 451.

[174] Ibid., pp. 451-452.

[175] Ibid., p. 458.

[176] Ibid., p. 440.

[177] Ibid., p. 442.

[178] Ibid., p. 428, emphases original.
[179] Ibid., pp. 428-429.
[180] Ibid., p. 429.
[181] Ibid., p. 428.
[182] Ibid., p. 429.
[183] Ibid., p. 450-451.
[184] Ibid., p. 457.
[185] Ryn, Claes. *A Common Human Ground: Universality and Particularity in a Multicultural World* (Columbia: University of Missouri Press, 2003), p. 49. Ryn's labor in this area has been tireless. In some crucial respects, his conclusions dovetail with the thesis for which I have been arguing. In some others, this is not evident. Still, in the interest of both space constraints as well as the focus of this paper, the just treatment to which Ryn's work is entitled must for now be deferred.
[186] Edmund Burke, "Reflections on the Revolution in France," in *The Portable Edmund Burke*, ed. Isaac Kramnick (New York: Penguin Books, 1999), p. 437.
[187] Thomas Aquinas, "Summa Contra Gentiles, Book One, Chapters 9-14," in *Thomas Aquinas: Selected Writings,* ed. Ralph McInerny (London: Penguin Books, 1998), p. 245.
[188] Kekes, John. *The Case for Conservatism* (Ithaca: Cornell University Press, 2001).
[189] Immanuel Kant. *Critique of Pure Reason,* eds. Guyer, Paul and Allen W. Wood (Cambridge: Cambridge University Press, 1999).
[190] Edmund Burke, "Reflections on the Revolution in France," in *The Portable Edmund Burke,* ed. Isaac Kramnick (New York: Penguin Books, 1999), p. 429.
[191] Ibid., p. 417.
[192] Ibid., p. 441.
[193] Ibid., p. 440, emphasis original.
[194] Ibid., p. 441.
[195] MacIntyre, Alasdair. *After Virtue* 2nd ed. (Indiana: University of Notre Dame Press, 1984), pp. 69-70.
[196] Edmund Burke, "Reflections on the Revolution in France," in *The Portable Edmund Burke,* ed. Isaac Kramnick (New York: Penguin Books, 1999), p. 417.
[197] Authors Joseph Conti, Stan Faryna, and Brad Stetson are among

those who have contributed in no small measure to the notion that all blacks who repudiate the prevailing racial orthodoxy are adherents of "black conservatism." See their *Black and Right: The Bold New Voice of Black Conservatism in America* (Westport, Connecticut: Praeger, 1997). Also, consult Conti and Stetson's, *Challenging the Civil Rights Establishment: Profiles of a New Black Vanguard* (Westport, Connecticut: Praeger, 1993). The former is a study of black rightists like Jesse Lee Peterson, Larry Elder, and Deroy Murdock who are by and large public figures accustomed to addressing popular audiences. The latter text, in contrast, exposits and analyzes the thought of such scholarly figures as Thomas Sowell, Shelby Steele, Glenn Loury, and Robert L. Woodson.

[198] A few remarks are in order. First, the provisional character of this threefold distinction between classical conservatism, classical liberalism, and neoconservatism should be duly noted from the outset. It should also be observed, however, that its value is rooted chiefly in this fact, for its open-endedness supplies a scheme or outline within which significant philosophical differences between thinkers typically linked together can be clearly delineated. Finally, while I am confident that I submit persuasive reasons for making the associations that I do between individual thinkers and political philosophical traditions, it must be admitted that my selections are not without some degree of arbitrariness. For this, though, I implore the reader to be merciful, for such arbitrariness I have tried to minimize and, besides, given the nature of the study, it is inescapable.

[199] Jerry Z. Muller's, *Conservatism: An Anthology of Social and Political Thought from David Hume to the Present* (Princeton: Princeton University Press, 1997) is an excellent survey of this 200 year intellectual tradition in which the reader is provided access to the work of the aforementioned thinkers.

[200] The disposition that I here refer to as "Rationalism" has alternatively been described by some of its opponents as "constructivism"(F.A.Hayek) and "gnosticism" (Eric Voeglin). See Hayeks, *Law, Legislation and Liberty*. 3 vols. (Chicago: The University of Chicago Press, 1973-1979), and Voeglin's, *The New Science of Politics* (Chicago: The University of Chicago Press, 1997).

[201] See Michael Oakeshott's insightful discussion of the relationship

between tradition and principle in the essay "Rationalism in Politics," in *Rationalism In Politics and Other Essays* (Indianapolis: Liberty Fund, 1962).

[202] Edmund Burke, "Reflections on the Revolution in France," in *The Portable Edmund Burke*. Ed. Isaac Kramnick (New York: Penguin Books, 1999), pp. 451-452.

[203] Ibid., p. 207.

[204] David Hume, Enquiries Concerning the Principles of the Understanding and the Principles of Morality. 3rd ed. Ed. P.H. Nidditch (Oxford: Oxford University Press, 1990), p. 288.

[205] Ibid., p. 172.

[206] David Hume, "Of the Original Contract," in *Essays Moral, Political, and Literary*. Revised ed. Ed. Eugene F. Miller (Indianapolis: Liberty Classics, 1987), p. 466.

[207] George S. Schuyler, "Negro-Art Hokum," in *Rac[e]ing To the Right*. Ed. Jeffrey B. Leak (Knoxville: University of Tennessee Press, 2001), p. 13.

[208] Ibid., p. 14.

[209] Ibid., p. 15.

[210] George S. Schuyler, "The Future of the American Negro," in *Rac[e]ing To the Right*. Ed. Jeffrey B. Leak (Knoxville: University of Tennessee Press, 2001), p. 109.

[211] Ibid., p. 110.

[212] George S. Schuyler, "The Case against the Civil Rights Bill," in *Rac[e]ing To the Right*. Ed. Jeffrey B. Leak (Knoxville: University of Tennessee Press, 2001), p. 97.

[213] Ibid., pp. 97-98.

[214] Ibid., p. 99, emphasis added.

[215] Ibid., p. 103.

[216] George S. Schuyler. *Black and Conservative: The Autobiography of George S. Schuyler* (New Rochelle: Arlington House Publishers, 1966), p. 332.

[217] For more (auto)biographical information on Sowell, see his *A Personal Odyssey* (New York: Simon & Schuster, 2000), as well as his *A Man of Letters* (New York: Encounter Books, 2007).

[218] Sowell. *Knowledge and Decisions*. (New York: Basic Books, 1996), p. 154.

[219] Ibid., p. 100.

[220] Ibid., p. 97.
[221] Ibid., p. 99.
[222] Ibid., p. 103.
[223] Ibid., p. 101.
[224] Thomas Sowell. *The Vision of the Anointed: Self-Congratulation as a Basis for Social Policy*. (New York: Basic Books, 1995), p. 118.
[225] Ibid., p. 119.
[226] Ibid., p. 110.
[227] Ibid., p. 113.
[228] John Locke. *Two Treatises of Government and A Letter Concerning Toleration*. Ed. Ian Shapiro (New Haven: Yale University Press, 2003), p. 101.
[229] Ibid., p. 102.
[230] Ibid., p. 141.
[231] Walter E. Williams. *Do the Right Thing* (Stanford: Hoover University Press, 1995), pp. vii-viii.
[232] Ibid., p. viii, emphasis original.
[233] Ibid., pp. viii-ix.
[234] Ibid., p. ix.
[235] Ibid., p. 40.
[236] Ibid., p. 57-58.
[237] Ibid., p. 71-72.
[238] Ibid., p. 72.
[239] For more on neoconservatism, see Douglas Murray's, *Neoconservatism: Why We Need It* (New York: Encounter Books, 2006), and Irving Kristol's, *Neoconservatism: The Autobiography of an Idea* (New York: The Free Press, 1995).
[240] Leo Strauss. *Natural Right and History*. 7th ed. (Chicago: University of Chicago Press, 1970), p. 2.
[241] Ibid., p. 13.
[242] Ibid., pp. 13-14.
[243] Francis Fukuyama, *America at the Crossroads: Democracy, Power, and the Neoconservative Legacy* (New Haven: Yale University Press, 2007), p. 48.
[244] Allan Bloom. *The Closing of the American Mind* (New York: Simon & Schuster, 1987), p. 330.
[245] Ibid., p. 153.
[246] Alan Keyes, "The Message of Freedom," in *Our Character, Our*

Future. Ed. George Grant (Grand Rapids: Zondervan Publishing House, 1996), p. 13.

[247] Ibid., p. 10.

[248] Alan Keyes, "The Crisis of Character," in *Our Character, Our Future.* Ed. George Grant (Grand Rapids: Zondervan Publishing House, 1996), p. 15.

[249] Ibid., p. 16.

[250] Ibid., p. 20-21.

[251] Alan Keyes, "The Human Conscience and Justice," in *Our Character, Our Future.* Ed. George Grant (Grand Rapids: Zondervan Publishing House, 1996), p. 113.

[252] Ibid., pp. 114-115.

[253] Ibid., p. 115.

[254] Ibid., p. 116.

[255] Ibid., p. 115.

[256] It is telling that no one ever speaks of, say, "black liberalism," even though the sympathies of most black intellectuals are with the liberal tradition. This, of course, to some extent, could account for why "black liberalism" is not among the expressions to be found in our political vocabulary. Yet I suspect that the apparent redundancy of "black liberalism" isn't the only reason for its conspicuous absence. The term "black conservatism" engenders, and is intended to engender, the notion that there is something intellectually disreputable and even, perhaps, morally questionable, about the thought of those black thinkers to whom it is ascribed. That this is so is evidenced by two considerations. First, no so-called "black conservative," to my knowledge, has ever identified him or herself as such. Some, in fact, and the "black conservative" on whose thought this study is based in particular, have expressly disavowed the label "black conservatism." Second, it is the enemies of "black conservatism" who coined this expression.

[257] Joseph G. Conti and Brad Stetson have written two studies of what they call "black conservatism." The first is a survey of black scholarly thought, while the second canvasses a range of popular writings. In *Challenging the Civil Rights Establishment: Profiles of a New Black Vanguard* (Westport: Praeger Publishers, 1993), the focus is on such "black conservative" thinkers as Thomas Sowell, Shelby Steele, Robert L. Woodson, and Glenn Loury. In *Black and Right* (Westport:

Praeger Publishers, 1997), Clarence Thomas, Jesse Lee Peterson, and Larry Elder are among the "black conservatives" discussed.

[258] Walter E. Williams, for example, a good friend and colleague of Thomas Sowell, and someone with whom the latter agrees on most racially oriented issues, is for the most part a liberal in the classical style, or what today is more fashionably referred to as a "libertarian." In *Do the Right Thing* (Stanford: Hoover Institution Press, 1995), Williams writes that "at the root of my values system is the principle of natural law" of the sort that the likes of John Locke, Thomas Jefferson, and Thomas Paine did much to defend and which was eventually enshrined in the Declaration of Independence (vii). "The first principle of natural law," Williams explains, "holds that each person owns himself." It is from this principle that our "rights to life, liberty, and property" are derived. Like Locke, Williams holds that government is legitimate only if it is rooted in consensual foundations. He subscribes to the idea of a "state of nature" from which free, equal, but "insecure" people flee and establish government for the sake of securing their rights. Sowell, as I will argue throughout this work, is not a classical liberal, at least not in the Lockean-Jeffersonian sense of that term. He never makes any of the rationalistic metaphysical appeals that Williams makes.

[259] Sowell recounts these features of his life in his memoirs. See his *A Personal Odyssey* (New York: Simon & Schuster, 2000). For a more abbreviated version of some of the same episodes, consult his *A Man of Letters* (New York: Encounter Books, 2007).

[260] Thomas Sowell, "What is 'Conservatism'?" in *Is Reality Optional?* (Stanford: Hoover Institution Press, 1993), p. 98.

[261] Ibid., p. 99.

[262] That the distinction between the formal and the substantive is anything but hard and fast is something of which I am well aware. Still, to concede this is far from conceding the uselessness of the distinction altogether. Just because it may be unclear in one situation or another whether a given position is substantive or "merely" formal doesn't mean that there aren't many situations when we can effortlessly, and without controversy, differentiate the formal from the substantive. It is no small feat, and more often than not, an impossible one, to specify how many grains of sand constitute a pile. Yet the simplest of children recognize a pile of sand when they see

one.

[263] For an excellent survey of classical conservative thought, see Jerry Z. Muller's *Conservatism: An Anthology of Social and Political Thought from David Hume to the Present* (Princeton: Princeton University Press, 1997). Muller makes this point that conservatism can't be understood in terms of the substance of the positions that individual conservatives have taken in different places and times, for "the institutions which conservatives have sought to conserve have varied, the major targets of conservative criticism have changed over time, and conservatism differs from one national context to another." While there are "substantive commitments" common to conservatives, an understanding of conservatism as a coherent intellectual tradition is to be gotten from focus on "an identifiable constellation of shared assumptions, predispositions, arguments," and "metaphors" that collectively "form a distinctive conservative pattern of social and political analysis" (p. xiii).

[264] Edmund Burke. *Reflections on the Revolution in France,* in *The Portable Edmund Burke.* Ed. Isaac Kramnick (New York: Penguin Books, 1999), pp. 451-452.

[265] F.A. Hayek. *The Fatal Conceit* (Chicago: The University of Chicago Press, 1988), p. 21.

[266] Ibid., p. 72.

[267] Ibid., p. 75.

[268] Michael Oakeshott. "Rationalisn in Politics," in *Rationalism in Politics and Other Essays* (Indianapolis: Liberty Fund, 1962), p. 12.

[269] Ibid., p. 15.

[270] Thomas Sowell. A Conflict of Visions: Ideological Origins of Political Struggles (New York: William Morrow, 1987).

[271] Thomas Sowell. The Vision of the Anointed: Self-Congratulation as a Basis for Social Policy (New York: Basic Books, 1995).

[272] Thomas Sowell. *A Conflict of Visions: Ideological Origins of Political Struggles* (New York: Basic Books, 1995). p. 40, emphasis original.

[273] Ibid., p. 42.

[274] Ibid., p. 41.

[275] Ibid., p. 45.

[276] Ibid., pp. 45-46.

[277] Michael Oakeshott. "Talking Politics," in *Rationalism in Politics and Other Essays* (Indianapolis: Liberty Fund, 1962), p. 454.

[278] Ibid., p. 455.
[279] Oakeshott explores this issue further in "The Rule of Law," in *On History and Other Essays* (Oxford: Basil Blackwell, 1983).
[280] Thomas Sowell. *The Quest for Cosmic Justice* (New York: The Free Press, 1999), p. 9.
[281] Ibid., p. 8, emphasis original.
[282] Ibid., p. 9.
[283] Ibid., pp. 4-5.
[284] Ibid., p. 5, emphasis added.
[285] Ibid., p. 13.
[286] Thomas Sowell. *Knowledge and Decisions* (New York: Basic Books, 1980), p. 369.
[287] Ibid., p. 331.
[288] Ibid., p. 369.
[289] Ibid., p. 370.
[290] Thomas Sowell. *A Conflict of Visions: Ideological Origins of Political Struggles* (New York: William Morrow, 1987), p. 68.
[291] Thomas Sowell. *The Vision of the Anointed: Self-Congratulation as a Basis for Social Policy* (New York: Basic Books, 1995), pp. 124-125, emphasis added.
[292] Michael Oakeshott. "On Being Conservative," in *Rationalism in Politics and Other Essays* (Indianapolis: Liberty Fund, 1962), p. 409.
[293] Ibid., p. 411.
[294] Thomas Sowell, *The Vision of the Anointed* (New York: Basic Books, 1995), p. 142.
[295] Ibid., p. 113, emphasis original.
[296] Michael Oakeshott, "Rationalism in Politics," in *Rationalism in Politics and Other Essays* (Indianapolis: Liberty Fund, 1962), p. 33.
[297] Thomas Sowell, *Civil Rights: Rhetoric or Reality?* (New York: William Morrow and Company, 1984), p. 14, emphasis original.
[298] Ibid., p. 15.
[299] Ibid., p. 23.
[300] Ibid., pp. 16-17.
[301] Ibid., p. 19.
[302] Ibid., p. 20.
[303] Ibid., p. 21.
[304] Ibid., p. 74, emphasis added.
[305] Ibid., p. 75.

[306] Ibid., pp. 84-85.
[307] Ibid., p. 85.
[308] Thomas Sowell, *Ethnic America* (New York: Basic Books, 1981), p. 219.
[309] Thomas Sowell, *The Economics and Politics of Race* (New York: William Morrow and Company, 1983), p. 107, emphasis added.
[310] Thomas Sowell, *The Vision of the Anointed* (New York: Basic Books, 1995), p. 57, emphasis original.
[311] Ibid., p. 58.
[312] Thomas Sowell, *Civil Rights: Rhetoric or Reality?* (New York: William Morrow and Company, 1984), pp. 22-23.
[313] Ibid., p. 23.
[314] Ibid., p. 32.
[315] Ibid., p. 30-31.
[316] Ibid., p. 32, emphasis original.
[317] Thomas Sowell, *Black Rednecks and White Liberals* (San Francisco: Encounter Books, 2005), 51, emphasis original.
[318] Ibid., pp. 50-51, emphasis original.
[319] Ibid., p. 51, emphasis original.
[320] Michael Oakeshott, *The Politics of Faith and the Politics of Scepticism.* Ed. Timothy Fuller (New Haven: Yale University Press, 1996).
[321] Thomas Sowell, *Is Reality Optional?And Other Essays?* (Stanford: Hoover Institution Press, 1993), p. 175.
[322] Ibid., p. 96.
[323] Thomas Sowell, *Knowledge and Decisions* (New York: Basic Books, 1980), p. 259.
[324] Thomas Sowell, *Is Reality Optional? And Other Essays* (Stanford: Hoover Institution Press, 1993), pp. 161-162.
[325] Thomas Sowell, *The Quest for Cosmic Justice* (New York: The Free Press, 1999), p. 156.
[326] Ibid., p. 170.
[327] *Rac[e]ing to the Right.* Ed. Jeffrey B. Leak (Knoxville: University of Tennessee Press, 2001).
[328] Ibid., p. ix.
[329] Ibid., p. xi.
[330] Ibid., p. xxxvi. Leak quotes E. Franklin Frasier's description of Schuyler.
[331] Cornel West's, *Hope on a Tightrope.* (Carlsbad: Hay House,

2008).
[332] Rac[e]ing to the Right. Ed. Jeffrey B. Leak (Knoxville: University of Tennessee Press, 2001), p. x.
[333] Ibid., p. xxxix.
[334] Ibid., p. xiii.
[335] Ibid., p. xli.
[336] Ibid., p. xxxiii.
[337] Michael Oakeshott, "Rationalism in Politics,", *Rationalism in Politics and Other Essays* (Indianapolis: Liberty Fund, 1962), pp. 14-15.
[338] Ibid., p. 15.
[339] Ibid., p. 12.
[340] Ibid., p. 15.
[341] Ibid., p. 11.
[342] Ibid., p. 16.
[343] Ibid., p. 15.
[344] Ibid., p. 40.
[345] Ibid., p. 33.
[346] Ibid., p. 41.
[347] Ibid., p. 8.
[348] Ibid., p. 11.
[349] Ibid., p. 10.
[350] Ibid., p. 11.
[351] Bruce Perry. *Malcolm: The Life of a Man Who Changed Black America* (Barrytown: Station Hill Press, 1992), pp. 175-176.
[352] Ibid., p. 232.
[353] Ibid., p. 363.
[354] Ibid., p. 424.
[355] Ibid., p. 203.
[356] Manning Marable. *Malcolm X: A Life of Reinvention* (New York: Viking Adult, 2011), pp. 264-265.
[357] That Malcolm fought for these causes is common knowledge. Manning Marable is among those of his biographers who does a particularly outstanding job of showing how the logic of Malcolm's evolving globalist vision—his "Pan-Africanism"—informed his support for them. See Marble's, *Malcolm X: A Life of Reinvention* (New York: Viking Adult, 2011).
[358] Cornel West. *Hope on a Tightrope* (Carlsbad: Hay House, 2008),

p. 43.
[359] Ibid., p. 44.
[360] Ibid., p. 45.
[361] Ibid., p. 47.
[362] Ibid., p. 46.
[363] Ibid., p. 50.
[364] Ibid., pp. 60-61.
[365] Ibid., p. 61.
[366] Edmund Burke, "Reflections on the Revolution in France," in *The Portable Edmund Burke*. Ed. Isaac Kramnick (New York: Penguin Books, 1999), pp. 451-452.
[367] Jerry Z. Muller's, *Conservatism: An Anthology of Social and Political Thought from David Hume to the Present* (Princeton: Princeton University Press, 1997).
[368] Edmund Burke, "Reflections on the Revolution in France," in *The Portable Edmund Burke*. Ed. Isaac Kramnick (New York: Penguin Books, 1999), p. 451.
[369] Ibid., p. 452.
[370] Michael Oakeshott, "Rationalism in Politics," in *Rationalism in Politics and Other Essays* (Indianapolis: Liberty Fund, 1962), p. 12.
[371] Edmund Burke, "Reflections on the Revolution in France," in *The Portable Edmund Burke*. Ed. Isaac Kramnick (New York: Penguin Books, 1999). p. 417.
[372] Ibid., p. 440.
[373] Ibid., p. 443.
[374] Ibid., p. 442.
[375] Ibid., p. 441.
[376] For his complete biography, see George S. Schuyler's, *Black and Conservative: The Autobiography of George S. Schuyler* (New Rochelle: Arlington House Publishers, 1966).
[377] Black scholar of religion and author of the first study of the Nation of Islam, C. Eric Lincoln, and famed black novelist, James Baldwin.
[378] George S. Schuyler, "The Black Muslims in America," in *Rac[e]ing to the Right*. Ed. Jeffrey Leak (Knoxville: University of Tennessee Press, 2001), p. 74.
[379] Ibid., emphasis added. Incidentally, C. Eric Lincoln conceded that Schuyler was correct on this score.

[380] Ibid., pp. 81-82.
[381] Ibid., p. 82.
[382] Ibid., p. 83.
[383] George S. Schuyler, "The Future of the American Negro," in *Rac[e]ing to the Right*. Ed. Jeffrey Leak (Knoxville: University of Tennessee Press, 2001), p. 111.
[384] George S. Schuyler, "The Case Against the Civil Rights Bill," in *Rac[e]ing to the Right*. Ed. Jeffrey Leak (Knoxville: University of Tennessee Press, 2001). p. 98.
[385] George S. Schuyler, "The Rising Tide of Black Racism," in *Rac[e]ing to the Right*. Ed. Jeffrey Leak (Knoxville: University of Tennessee Press, 2001), p. 106.
[386] Ibid., pp. 107-108.
[387] Ibid., p. 108.
[388] George S. Schuyler, "Negro-Art Hokum," in *Rac[e]ing to the Right*. Ed. Jeffrey Leak (Knoxville: University of Tennessee Press, 2001), p. 13.
[389] Ibid., p. 14.
[390] Ibid., p. 15.
[391] Ibid., p. 14.
[392] Ibid., p. 15.
[393] George S. Schuyler, "The Case Against the Civil Rights Bill," in *Rac[e]ing to the Right*. Ed. Jeffrey Leak (Knoxville: University of Tennessee Press, 2001), p. 97, emphasis original.
[394] Ibid., pp. 97-98.
[395] Ibid., p. 103.
[396] *Rac[e]ing to the Right*. Ed. Jeffrey B. Leak (Knoxville: University of Tennessee Press, 2001), p. x.
[397] Ibid.
[398] Jn. 21: 25. *The New Revised Standard Version: Catholic Edition* (Nashville: The New Revised Standard Version, 1993), p. 116.
[399] This is not mere hyperbole. Duane "Dogg the Bounty Hunter" Chapman is a convicted murderer who became a reality TV celebrity. When, however, he was heard on a recording using a racially-charged epithet regarding blacks, Chapman spared no tears as he threw himself at the mercy of the media. From one talk show to the next, Chapman appeared with his black pastor as he pleaded with the public to forgive him his transgression—not the

transgression of murder, mind you, but that of using this mother of all racial slurs—and accept that he is *not* a "racist." Beyond this, one need only consider such recent examples as those of chef celebrity Paula Deen, veteran talk radio host Don Imus, and LA Clippers owner Don Sterling to see just how swiftly even the most immensely successful of careers have been brought to a screeching halt because the accused had been suspected of harboring "racist" thoughts.

[400] Conti, Joseph G., Faryna, Stan, and Brad Stetson, eds. *Black and Right: The Bold New Voice of Black Conservatives in America* (Westport: Praeger, 1997), p. 66.

[401] Ibid., p. 67.

[402] Ibid., p. 66.

[403] Oakeshott, Michael. *On Human Conduct* (London: Oxford University Press, 1975), p. 72.

[404] Rachels, James, "Ethical Egoism," in eds. Fieser, James and Louis Pojman. *Introduction to Philosophy: Classical and Contemporary Readings*. 4th edition (New York: Oxford University Press, Inc., 2008), p. 556.

[405] Ibid., pp. 556-557.

[406] Ibid., p. 556.

[407] D'Souza, Dinesh. *The End of Racism: Principles for A Multiracial Society* (New York: Simon & Schuster Inc., 1995), p. 27.

[408] Quoted in Sowell, Thomas. *Black Rednecks and White Liberals* (San Francisco: Encounter Books, 2005), p. 167.

[409] D'Souza, Dinesh. *The End of Racism: Principles for a Multiracial Society* (New York: Simon & Schuster Inc., 1995), p. 28, emphasis added.

[410] Wasserstrom, Richard, "On Racism and Sexism: Realities and Ideals," in ed. Arthur, John. *Morality and Moral Controversies*: *Readings in Moral, Social, and Political Philosophy*. 7th edition (Upper Saddle River: Pearson Prentice Hall, 2005), p. 563.

[411] Young, Iris Marion, "Social Movements and the Politics of Difference," in ed. Arthur, John. *Morality and Moral Controversies: Readings in Moral, Social, and Political Philosophy*. 7th edition (Upper Saddle Rivers: Pearson Prentice Hall, 2005), p. 572.

[412] Ibid., p. 573.

[413] Sowell, Thomas. The Vision of the Anointed: Self-Congratulation as a Basis for Social Policy (New York: Basic Books, 1995), p. 35

[414] Ibid., pp. 35-36.
[415] Ibid., p. 36.
[416] Sowell, Thomas. *Civil Rights: Rhetoric or Reality* (New York: Harper Collins, 1984), pp. 80-81.
[417] Ibid., p. 81, emphasis original.
[418] Bonilla-Silva, Eduard. *Racism Without Racists* (Lanham: Rowman & Littlefield Publishers, 2006).
[419] For an interesting discussion "useless knowledge," see Alan Watts', *Tao: The Watercourse Way* (New York: Random House), 1975.
[420] Chasmar, Jessica, "Saint Louis University Removes 'Racist' Statue of Catholic Priest Praying Over Native Americans," The Washington Times, May 2015,
http://www.washingtontimes.com/news/2015/may/27/saint-louis-university-removes-racist-statue-of-pr/
(accessed June 1, 2015)
[421] That's correct: The conservative's objections notwithstanding, academics don't so much "indoctrinate" their students as they *reinforce* the prejudices that students have imbibed from the culture, from Hollywood, their primary and secondary education, popular music, etc. The ideology in which college students are trained (not *educated*) has been in the air that they've been breathing all of their lives.
[422] Kazuo, Rodrigo and Meg Perret, "Occupy the Syllabus," The Daily Californian, January 2015,
http://www.dailycal.org/2015/01/20/occupy-syllabus/
(accessed September 30, 2015)
[423] Hasson, Peter, "Bias-Free Language Guide Claims the word 'American' is Problematic," Campus Reform, July 2015,
http://www.campusreform.org/?ID=6697
(accessed September 30, 2015)
[424] Brindley, Michael, "UNH President 'Troubled' By School's Bias-Free Language Guide," New Hampshire Public Radio, July 2015,
http://nhpr.org/post/unh-president-troubled-schools-bias-free-language-guide
(accessed September 30, 2015)
[425] University of California, Office of the Presidency, "Recognizing Micro-Aggressions and the Messages that they Send,"

http://www.ucop.edu/academic-personnel-programs/_files/seminars/Tool_Recognizing_Microaggressions.pdf (accessed September 30, 2015)
[426] Hannah Arendt, "Thinking and Moral Consideration: A Lecture," in *Social Research,* vol. 38, no. 3 (Fall 1971): p. 418.
[427] Ibid. p. 435.
[428] Ibid. p. 431.
[429] Ibid. p. 438.
[430] Ibid. p. 435.
[431] Ibid. pp. 434-435.
[432] Ibid. p. 441
[433] Ibid. p. 442
[434] "Emily Post Quotations," at emilypost.com, August, http://www.emilypost.com/everyday-manners/guidelines-for-living/454-emily-post-quotations (accessed August 21, 2015)
[435] Anna Post, Post, Lizzie, Post, Peggy, & Senning Post, Daniel, eds. *Emily Post's Etiquette,* 18th edition. (New York: Harper Collins, 2011), p. 7, emphasis added.
[436] Ibid. p. 8.
[437] Ibid. pp. 9-10.
[438] Ibid. p. 6.
[439] Oakeshott, Michael, "Talking Politics", in *Rationalism in Politics and Other Essays* (Indianapolis: Liberty Fund, 1962), p. 454.